Dual Mania (Music from the Original Soundtrack Album)

Piano/Guitar/Chords – Sheet Music Book

BOOKS BY CAT ELLINGTON

REVIEWS BY CAT ELLINGTON: THE COMPLETE ANTHOLOGY, VOL. 1

REVIEWS BY CAT ELLINGTON: THE COMPLETE ANTHOLOGY, VOL. 2

THE MAKING OF DUAL MANIA: FILMMAKING CHICAGO STYLE

REVIEWS BY CAT ELLINGTON – THE COMPLETE ANTHOLOGY LIMITED EDITION HOLIDAY GIFT SET (BOOKS 1 & 2)

REVIEWS BY CAT ELLINGTON: THE COMPLETE ANTHOLOGY, VOL. 3

MORE IMAGINATIVE THAN ORDINARY SPEECH: THE POETRY OF CAT ELLINGTON

REVIEWS BY CAT ELLINGTON: A TRILOGY OF UNIQUE CRITIQUES #1

MEMOIRS IN GOGYOHKA: A BOOK OF SHORT POEMS AND MEMOIRS

YOU CAN QUOTE ME ON THAT: A COLLECTION OF QUOTES BY CAT ELLINGTON

REVIEWS BY CAT ELLINGTON: THE COMPLETE ANTHOLOGY, VOL. 4

REVIEWS BY CAT ELLINGTON: THE COMPLETE ANTHOLOGY, VOL. 5

REVIEWS BY CAT ELLINGTON: THE COMPLETE ANTHOLOGY, VOL. 6

I DO: SHEET MUSIC

THE BOOK OF US: SHEET MUSIC

I'M STILL IN LOVE: SHEET MUSIC

SOMETHING IN YOUR EYES: SHEET MUSIC

GETT OUT: SHEET MUSIC

THE FIVE-STAR REVIEW: A COLLECTION OF CAT ELLINGTON'S TOP-RATED BOOK REVIEWS FROM 1981-2021

STRIKE A PROSE: A FRAMEWORK OF MEMORIES AND COMMENTARIES IN POETRY

REVIEWS BY CAT ELLINGTON: A TRILOGY OF UNIQUE CRITIQUES #2

REVIEWS BY CAT ELLINGTON: THE COMPLETE ANTHOLOGY, VOL. 7

REVIEWS BY CAT ELLINGTON: THE COMPLETE ANTHOLOGY, VOL. 8

REVIEWS BY CAT ELLINGTON: THE COMPLETE ANTHOLOGY, VOL. 9

REVIEWS BY CAT ELLINGTON: A TRILOGY OF UNIQUE CRITIQUES #3

DUAL MANIA (MUSIC FROM THE ORIGINAL SOUNDTRACK ALBUM) PIANO/GUITAR/CHORDS - SHEET MUSIC BOOK

THE COMPLETE WORKS: REVIEWS BY CAT ELLINGTON, BOOKS 1-9

Books by Joseph Strickland

THE MAKING OF DUAL MANIA: FILMMAKING CHICAGO STYLE

REVIEWS BY CAT ELLINGTON: THE COMPLETE ANTHOLOGY, VOL. 5

REVIEWS BY CAT ELLINGTON: A TRILOGY OF UNIQUE CRITIQUES #2

GETT OUT: SHEET MUSIC

DUAL MANIA (MUSIC FROM THE ORIGINAL SOUNDTRACK ALBUM)
PIANO/GUITAR/CHORDS - SHEET MUSIC BOOK

THE COMPLETE WORKS: REVIEWS BY CAT ELLINGTON, BOOKS 1-9

Dual Mania (Music from the Original Soundtrack Album)

Piano/Guitar/Chords – Sheet Music Book

Cat Ellington

With

Joseph Strickland

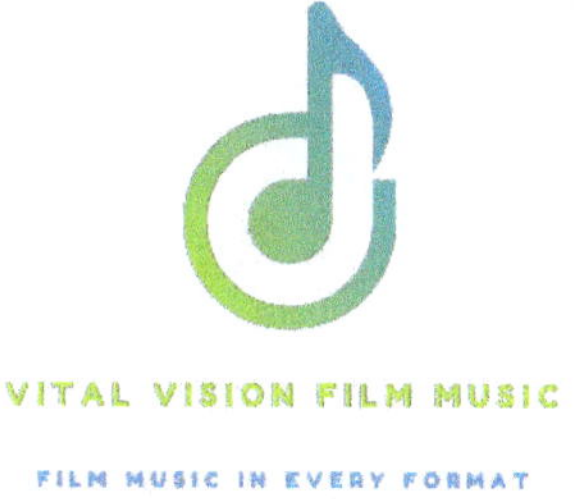

Chicago, Illinois

ISBN: 979-8-218-36812-8

ISMN: 979-0-800290-00-8

Library of Congress Control Number: 2024902443

Cover design by: Cheryl Brown

Vital Vision Records
Dark Planet Publishing
The Black Jaguar Music Company
The Cat Ellington Song Catalog
The Cat Ellington Sheet Music Collection
Dual Mania (The Original Motion Picture Soundtrack)
Instrumentals: Music from the Motion Picture Dual Mania

Published by Vital Vision Film Music
Chicago, Illinois, USA

Vital Vision Film Music, 2024

Printed in the U.S.A.

Introduction

Inspired by the music composed by the one-and-only Cat Ellington, Vital Vision Film Music presents *Dual Mania (Music from the Original Soundtrack Album) Piano/Guitar/Chords – Sheet Music Book*. The issue features the musical scores of songs written by Cat Ellington through The Black Jaguar Music Company, previously recorded with vocals by various artists.

Dual Mania (Music from the Original Soundtrack Album) Piano/Guitar/Chords – Sheet Music Book, includes the first five songs released from the Cat Ellington song catalog. These include the award-winning "I Do," "The Book Of Us," "I'm Still In Love," "Something In Your Eyes," and "Gett Out," the latter being the first work from the Heavy Metal collection of the song catalog.

This volume also includes original song synopses of the works created by Cat Ellington for her catalog's original Song Synopsis.

The Black Jaguar Music Company, the publisher of the Cat Ellington song catalog, provided the synopses and illustrations for this volume.

The five scores presented on these pages are for songs that appear (with vocals) on the soundtrack to the multi-award-winning feature film "Dual Mania," *Dual Mania (The Original Motion Picture Soundtrack)*, and on *Instrumentals: Music from the Motion Picture Dual Mania*, the EP composed by Cat Ellington & Joseph Strickland, produced by Cat Ellington, Princeton Brown, and Greg Schutte, and executive produced by Joseph Strickland.

—**Vital Vision Film Music**

"I DO"

Acoustic Grand Piano

I Do, the winner of the 2019 Vegas Movie Awards Award for Best Song, was written by Cat Ellington and performed by Minneapolis native Jaki Cavins for *Dual Mania (The Original Motion Picture Soundtrack)*. The track was co-produced by Cat Ellington and Princeton Brown for Vital Vision Records.

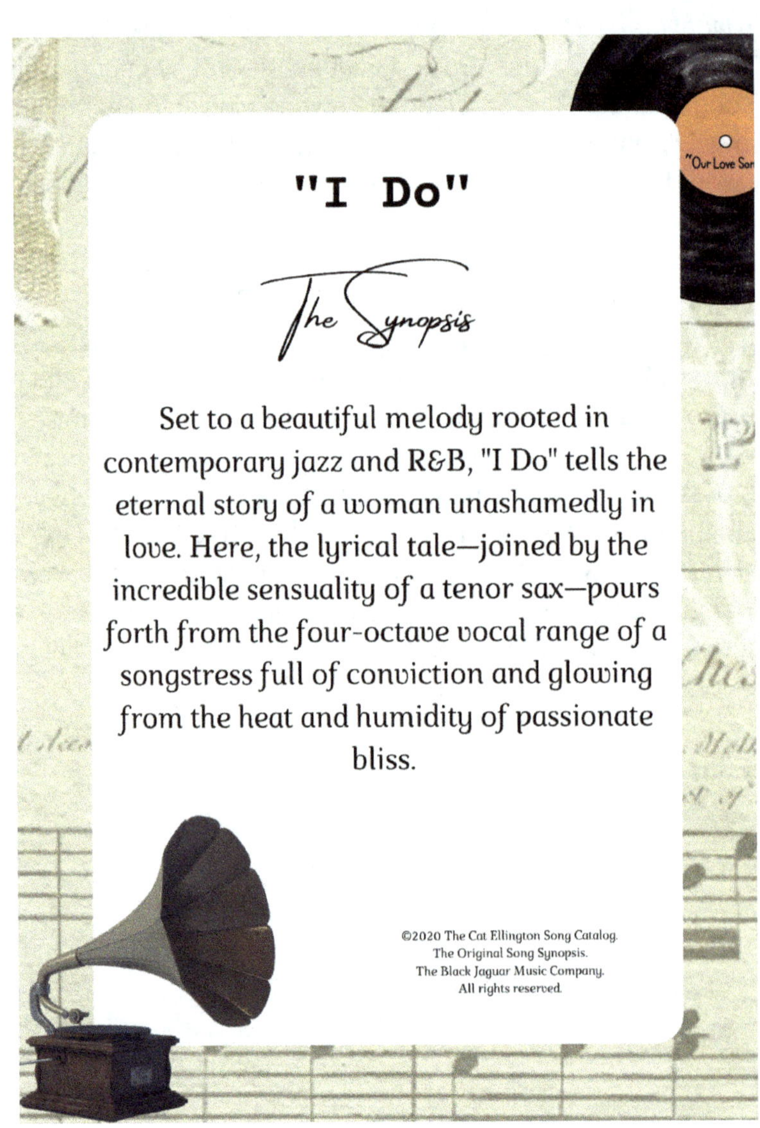

I DO (Acoustic Grand Piano)

Composers: Cat Ellington / Princeton Brown

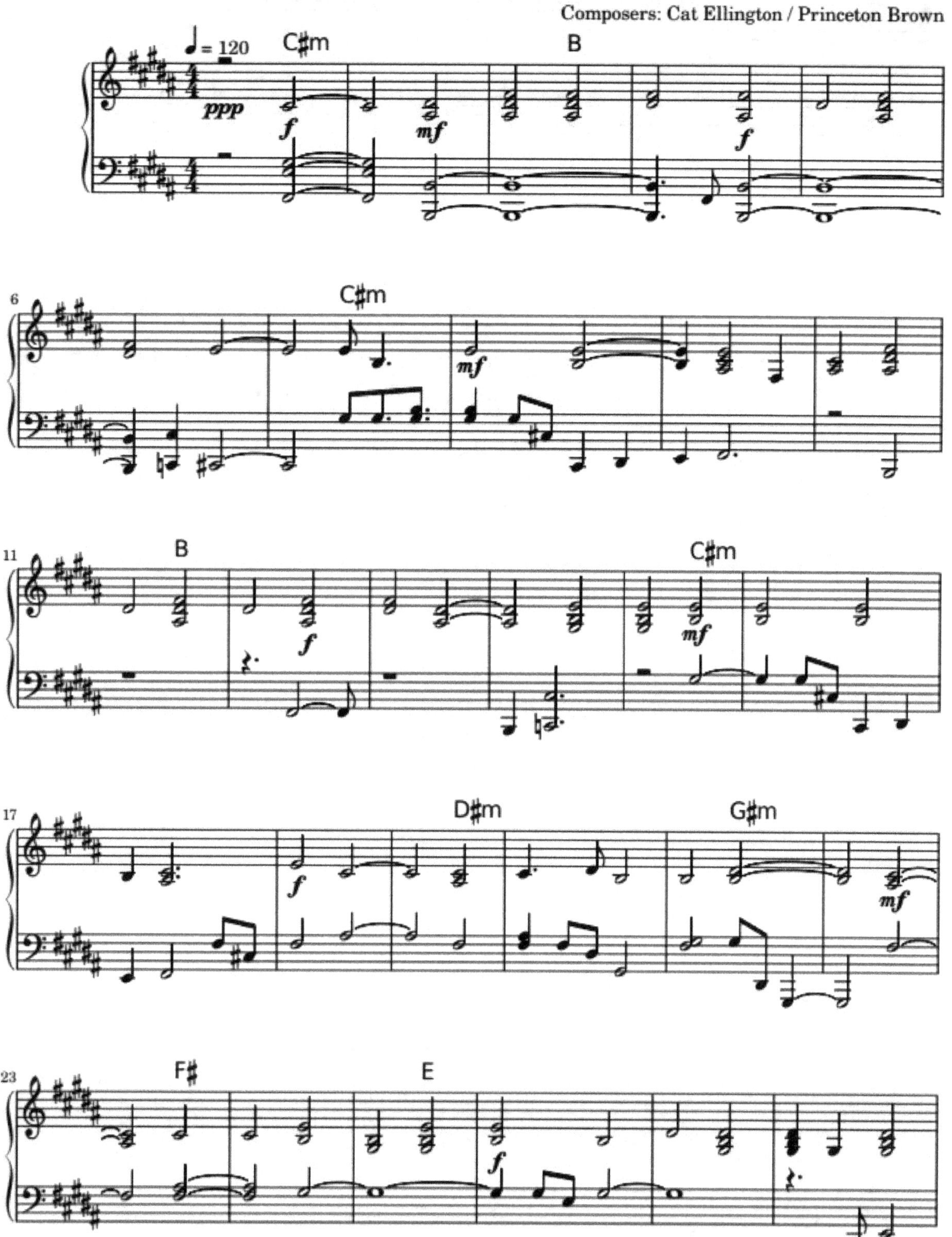

2

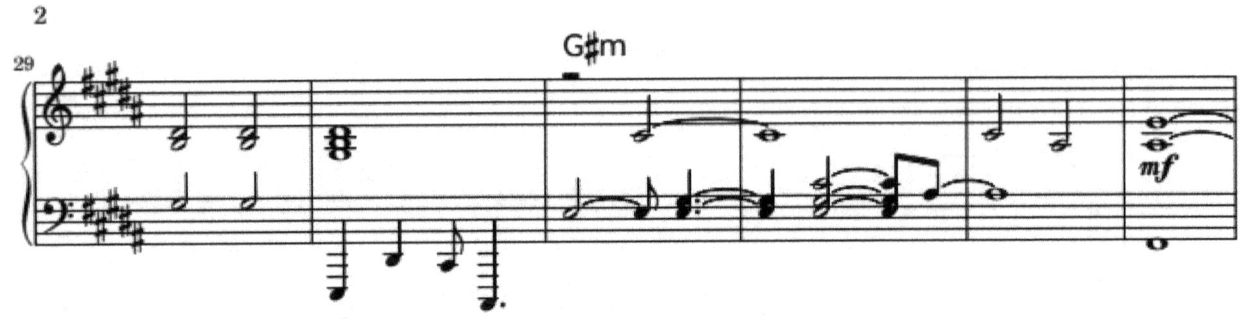

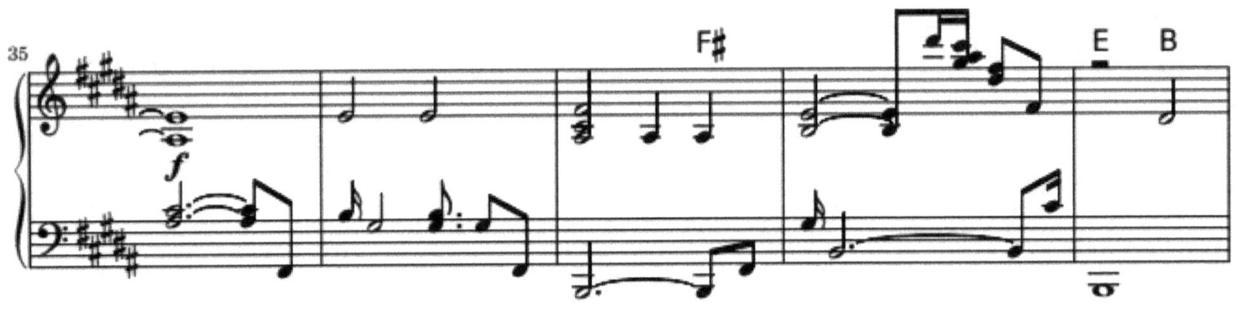

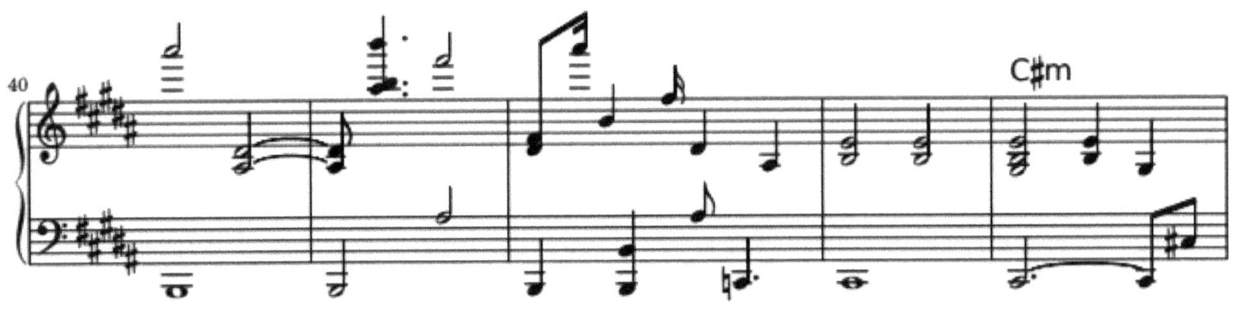

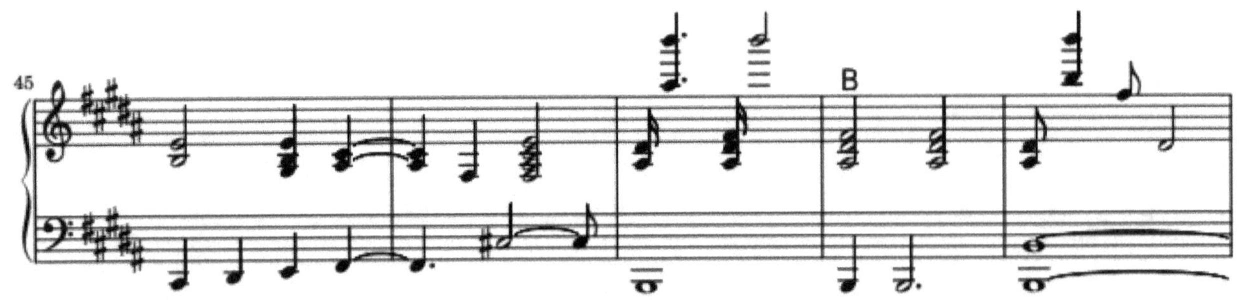

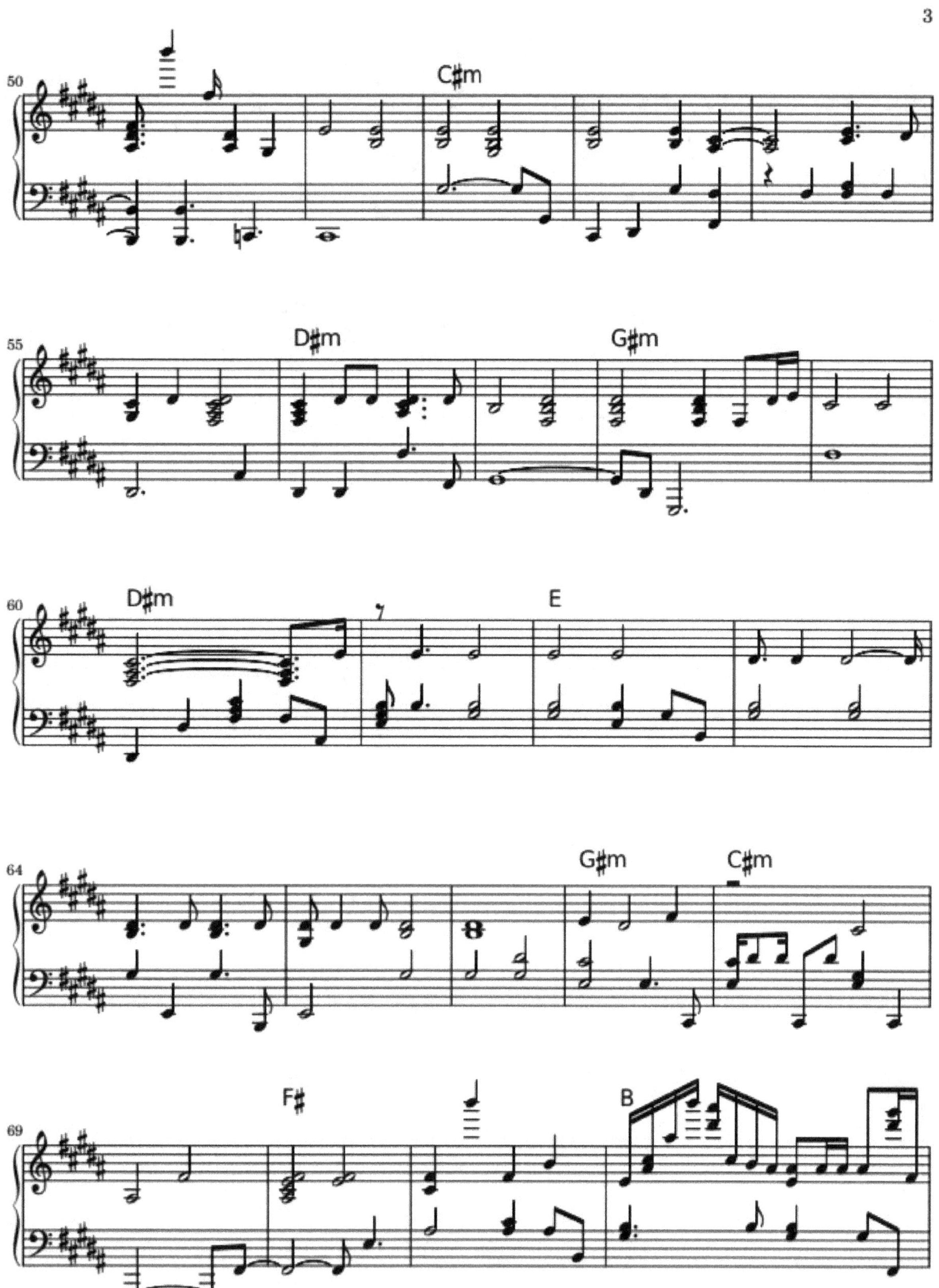

50
C♯m
55
D♯m
G♯m
60
D♯m
E
64
G♯m
C♯m
69
F♯
B

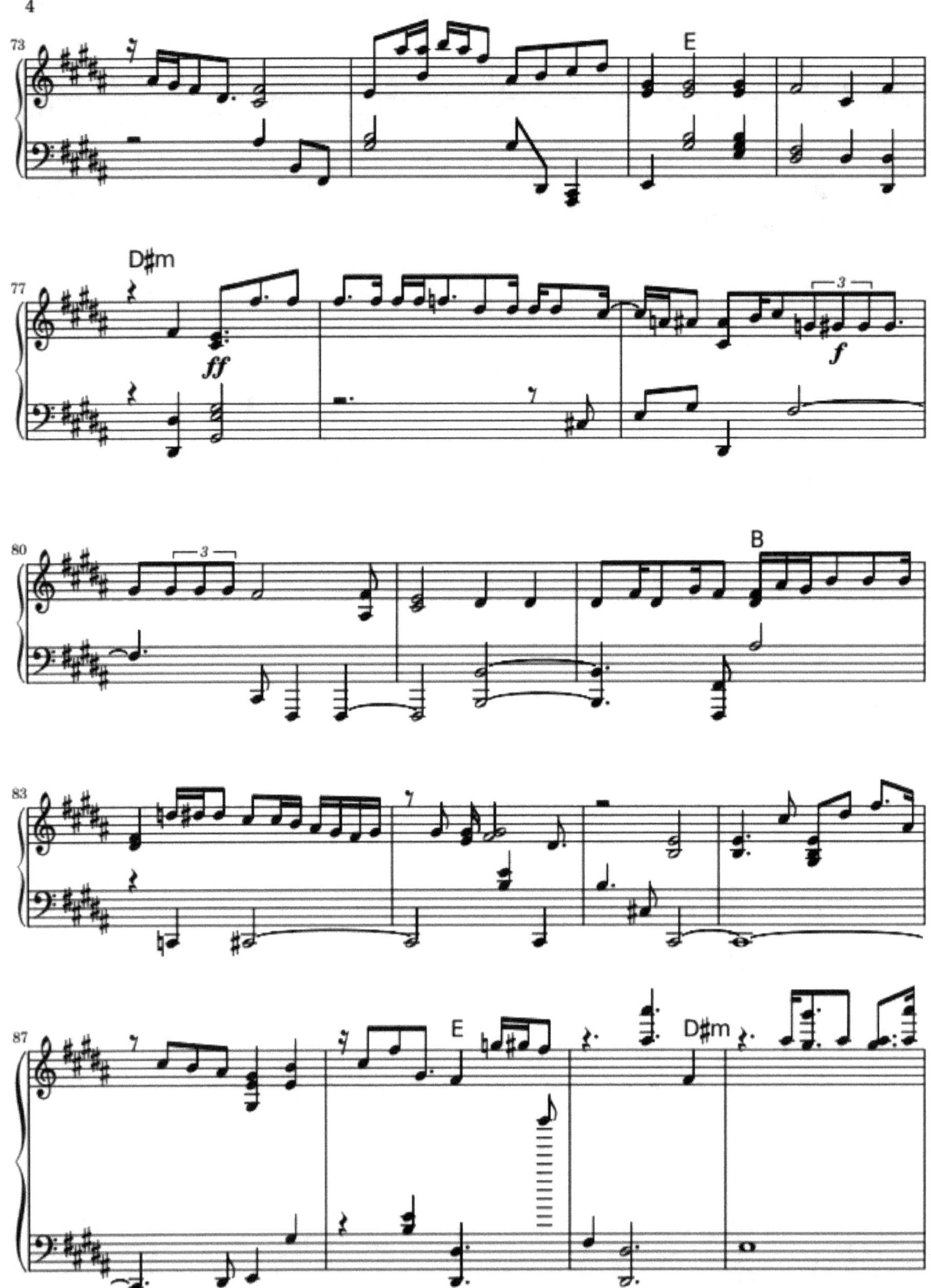
4
73
E
77
D♯m
ff
3
f
80
3
B
83
87
E
D♯m

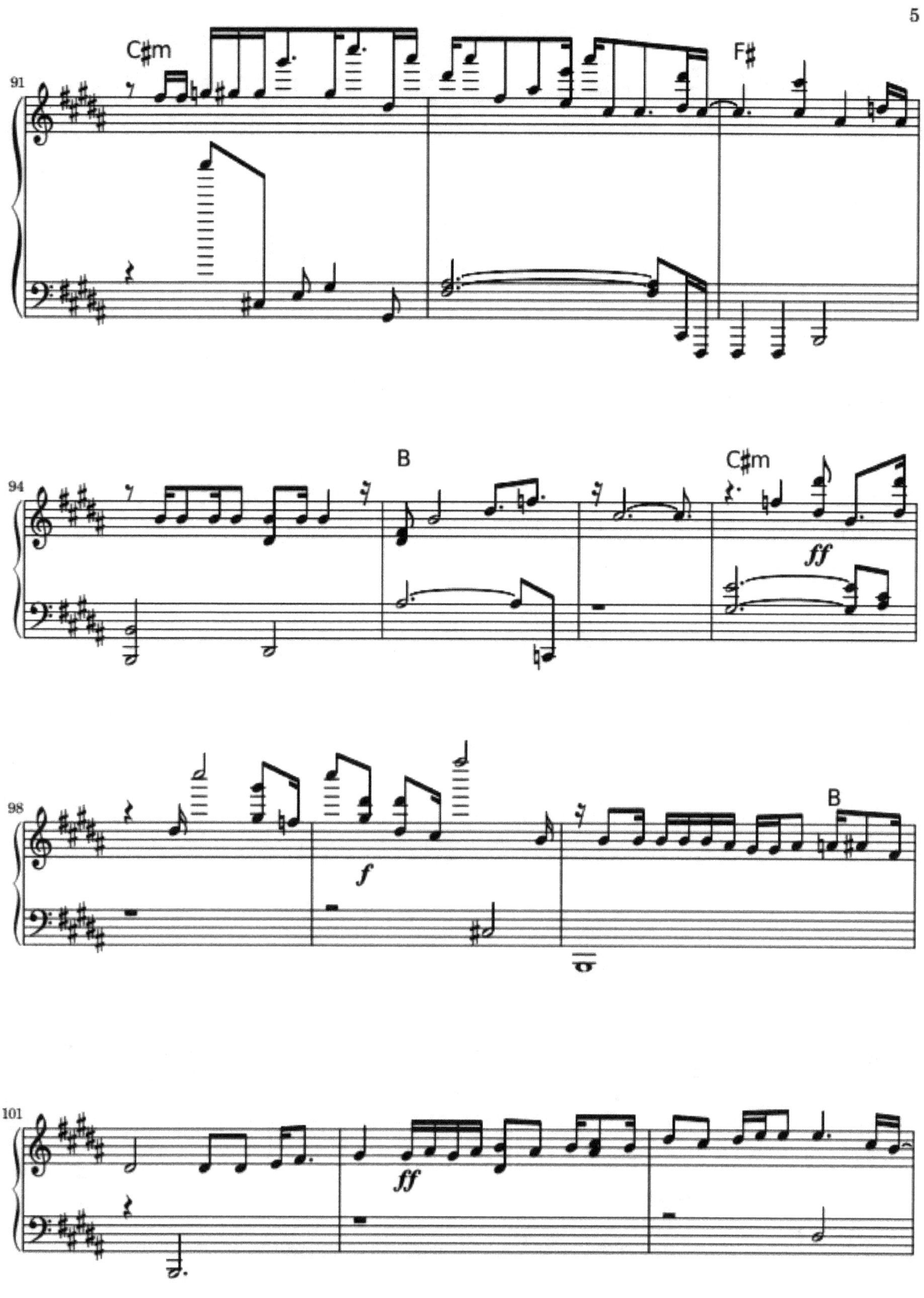

5

91
C♯m
F♯

94
B
C♯m
ff

98
B
f

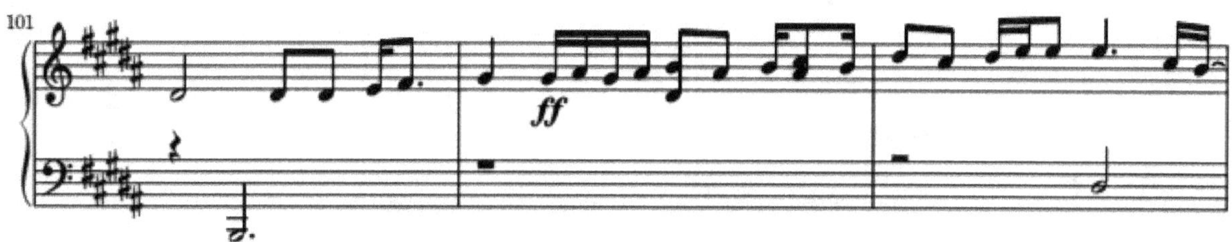

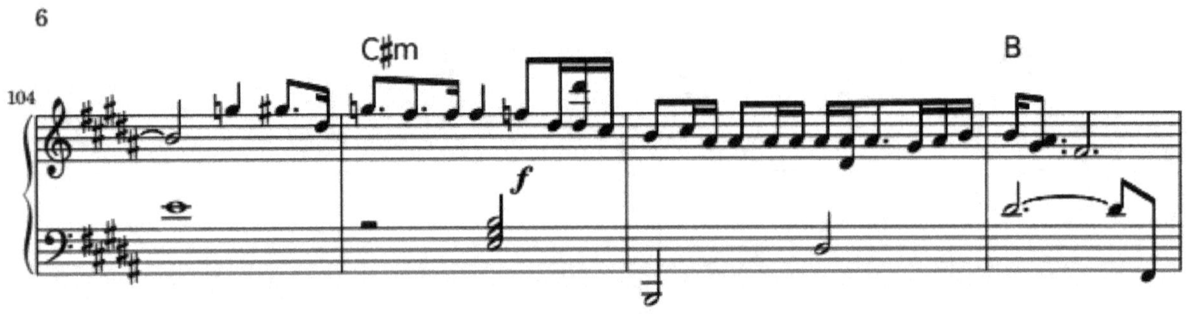
104
C♯m
B
f

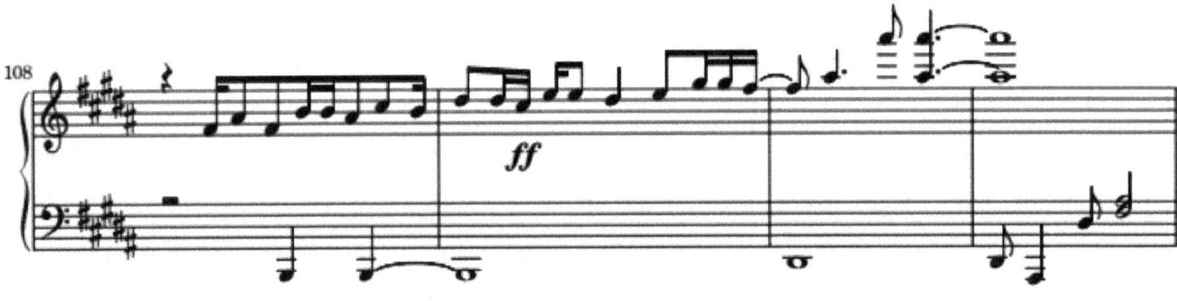
108
ff

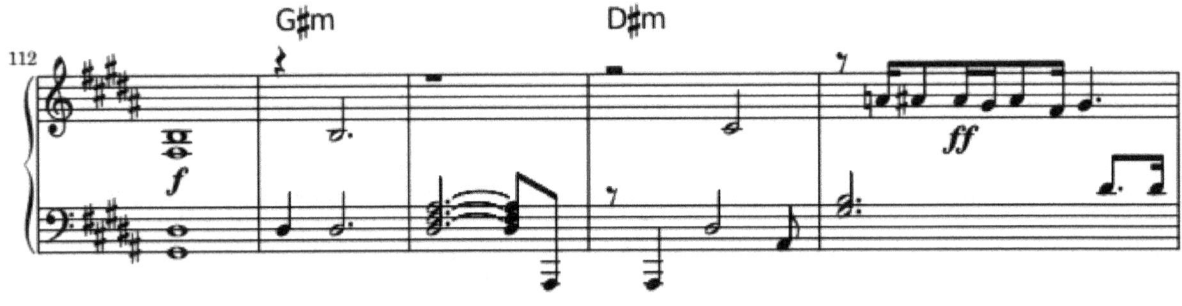
112
G♯m
D♯m
f
ff

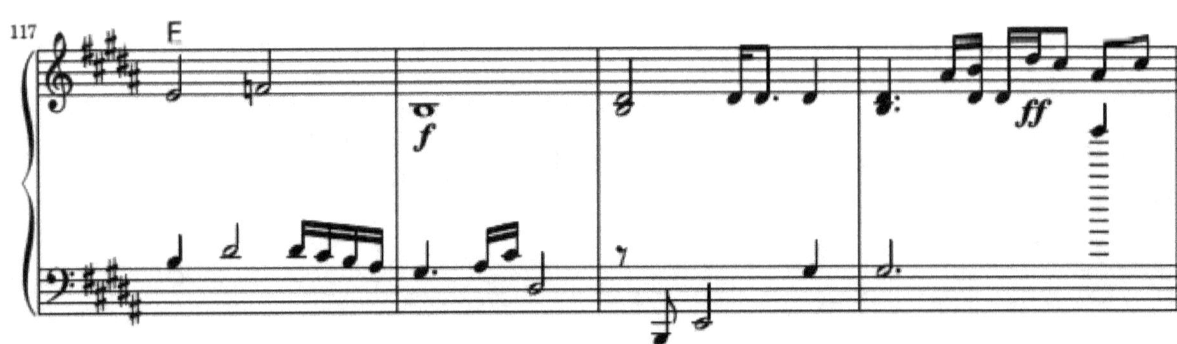
117
E
f
ff

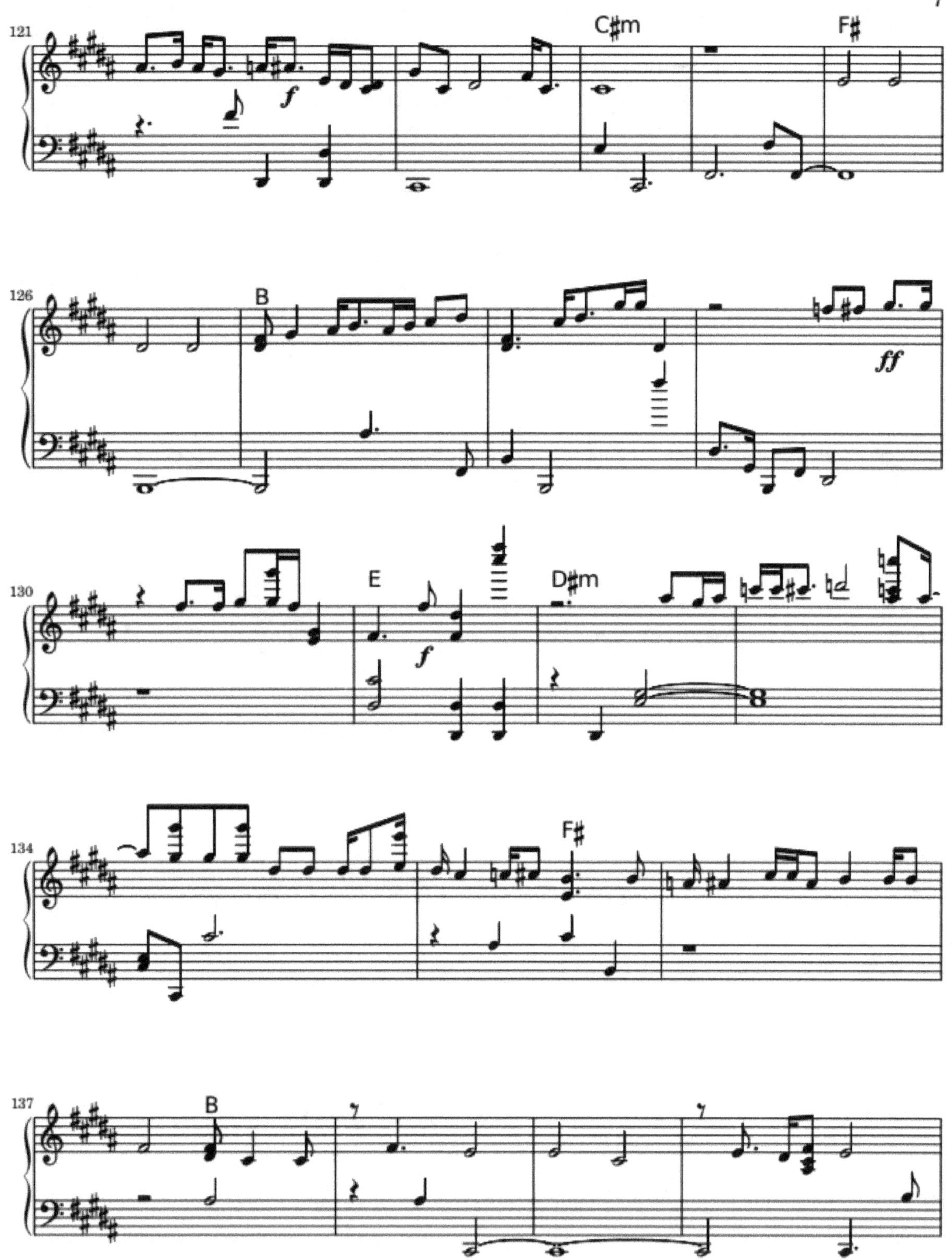
7
121
C♯m
F♯
f
126
B
ff
130
E
D♯m
f
134
F♯
137
B

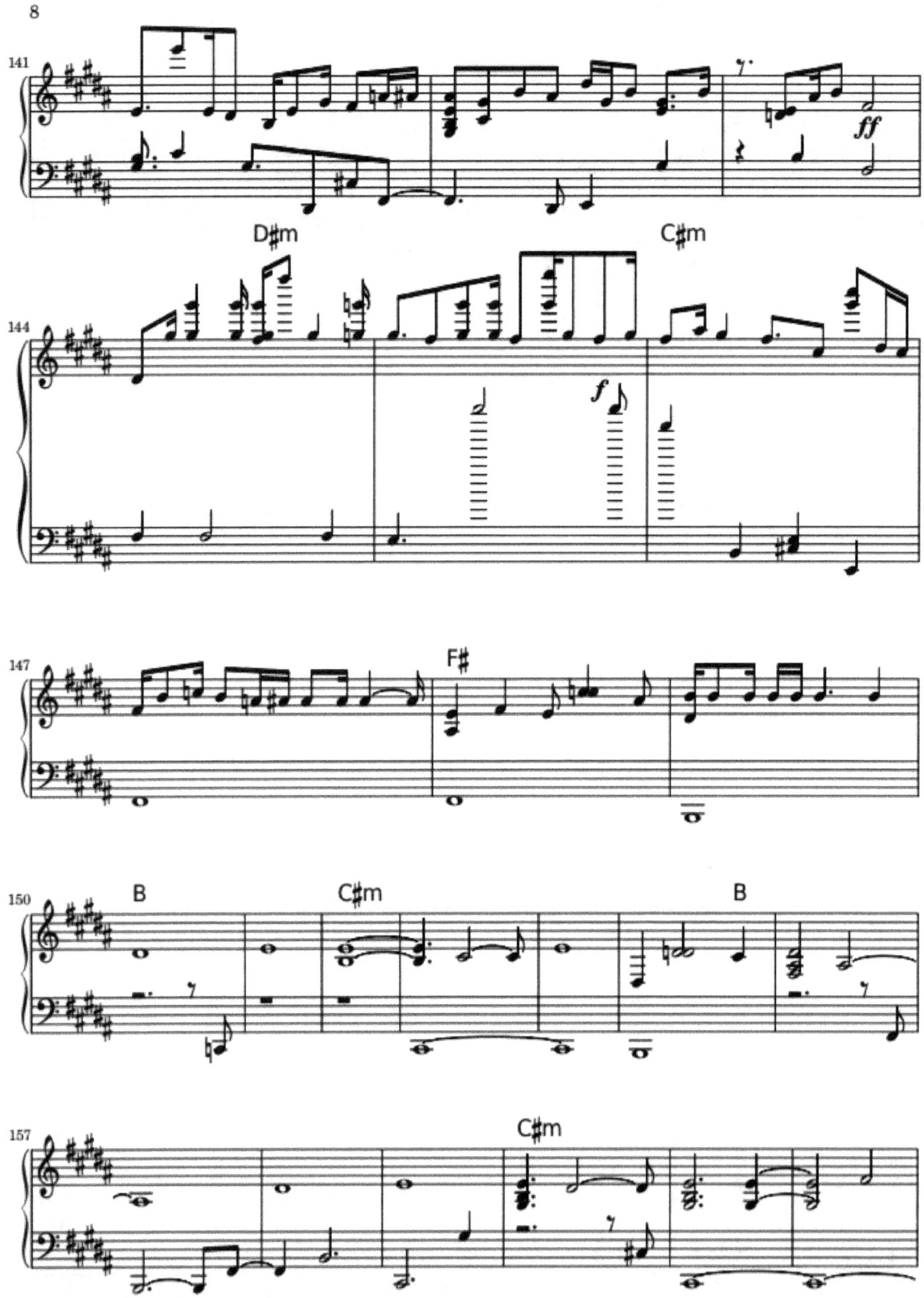
8
141
ff
144
D♯m
C♯m
f
147
F♯
150
B
C♯m
B
157
C♯m

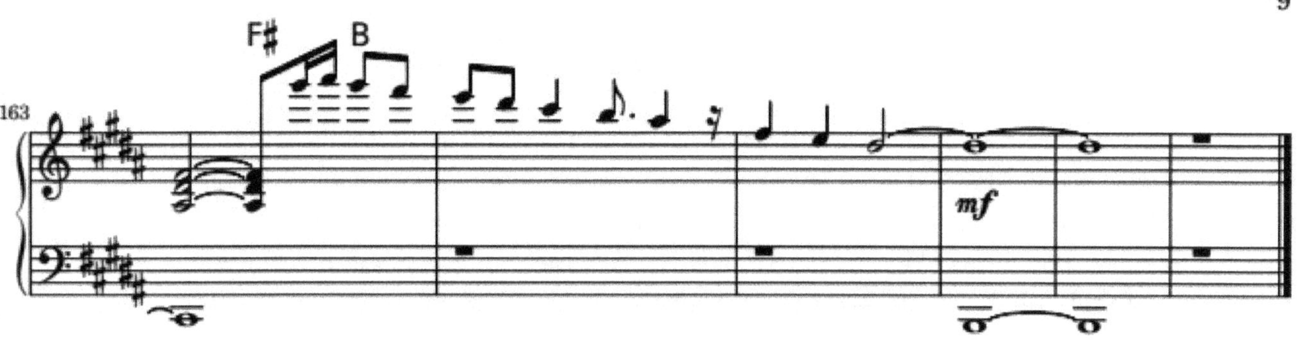
163
F♯
B
mf

"THE BOOK OF US"

Acoustic Grand Piano

A romantic ballad, *The Book of Us* is the second release from the Cat Ellington song catalog. The piece was written by Cat Ellington and performed by Minneapolis native Jaki Cavins for *Dual Mania (The Original Motion Picture Soundtrack)*. The track was co-produced by Cat Ellington and Princeton Brown for Vital Vision Records.

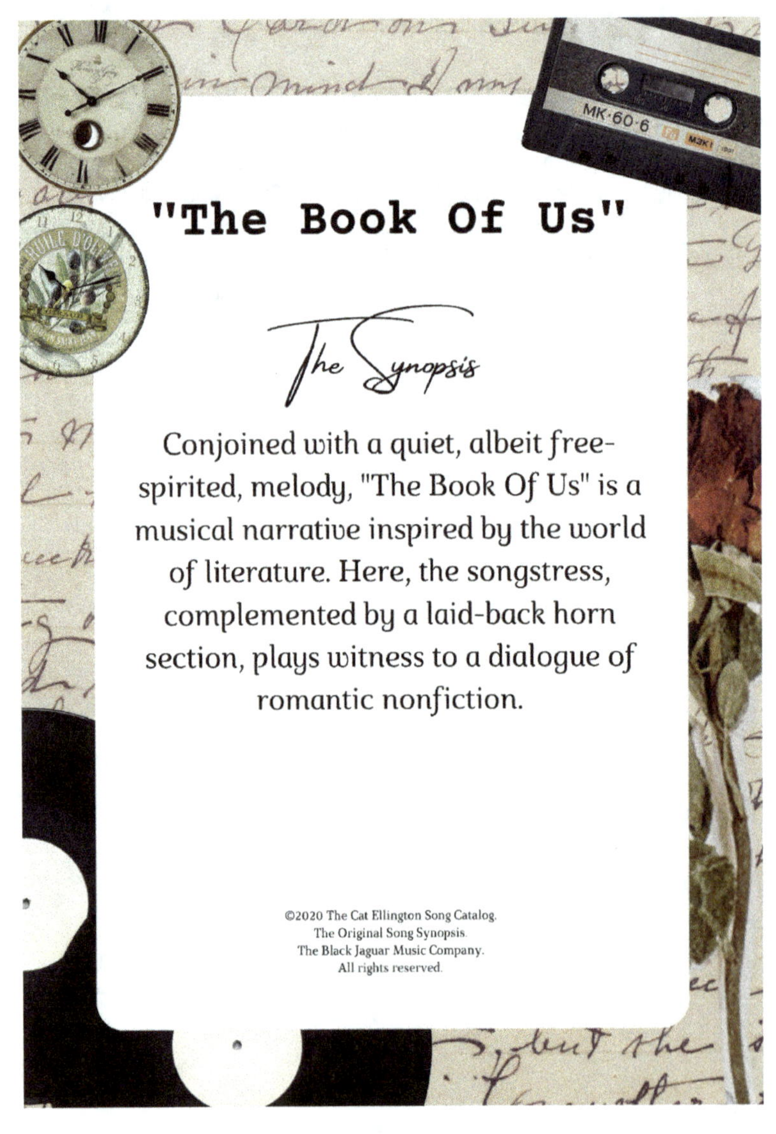

THE BOOK OF US (Acoustic Grand Piano)

Composers: Cat Ellington / Princeton Brown

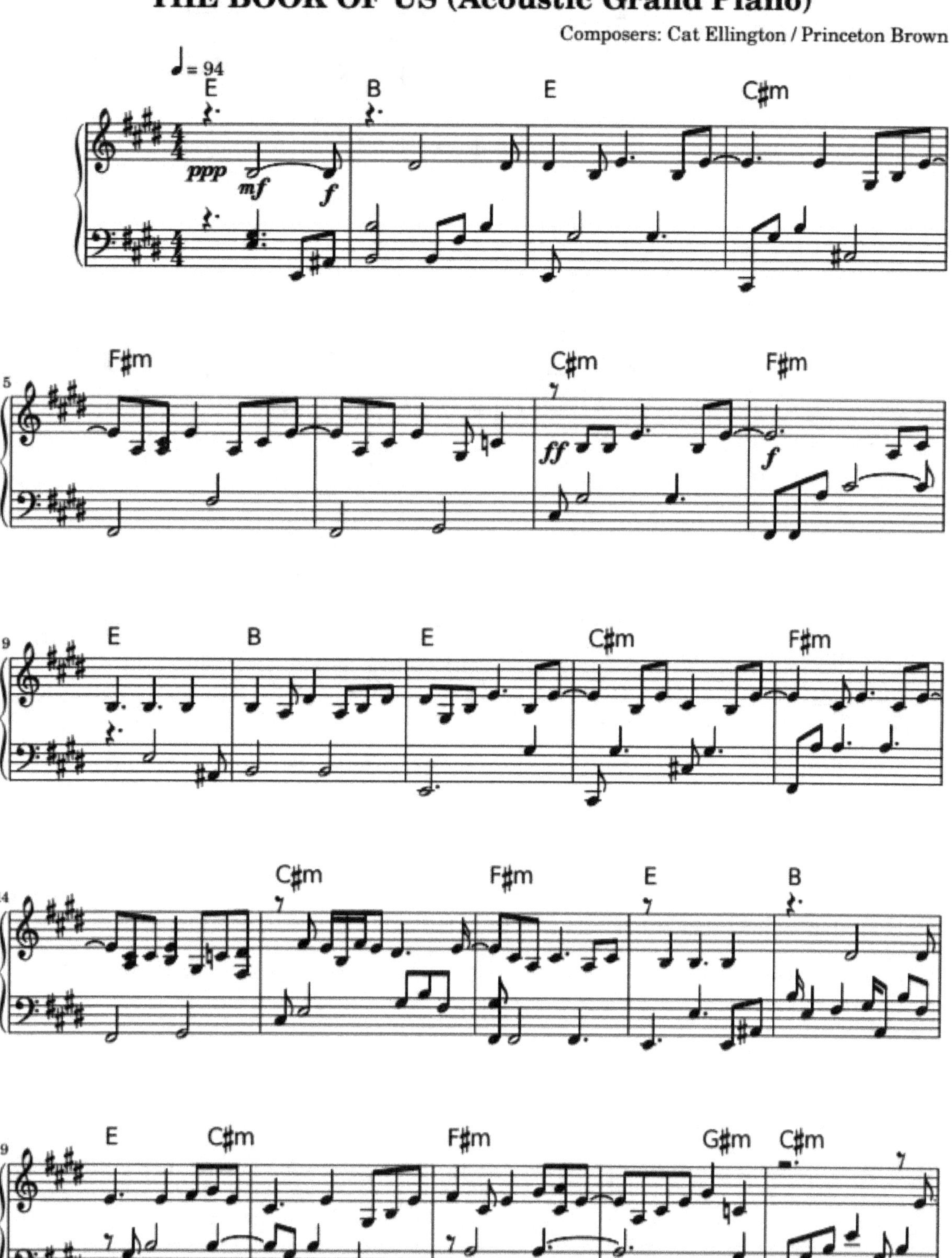

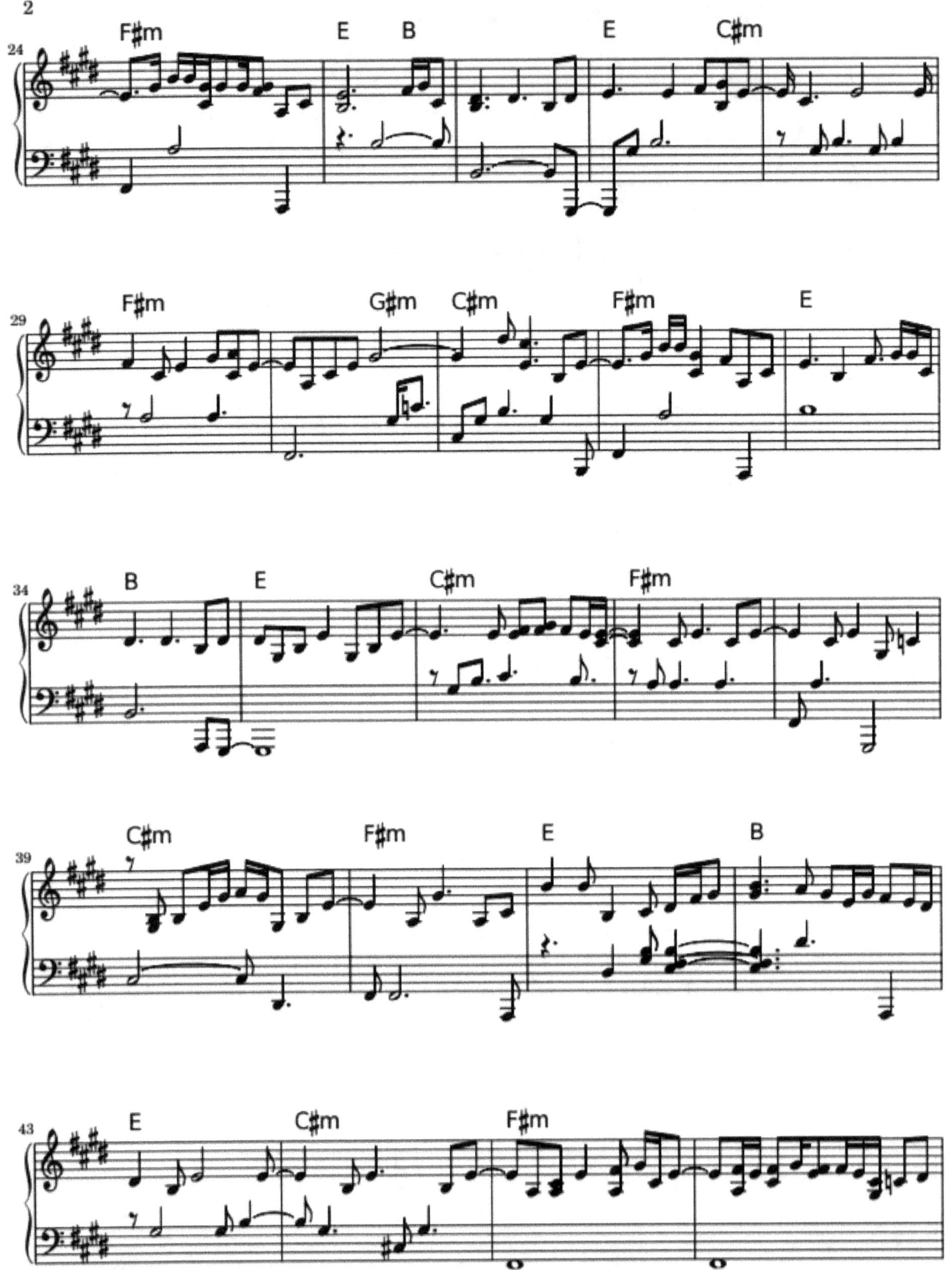
2
24
F♯m E B E C♯m
29
F♯m G♯m C♯m F♯m E
34
B E C♯m F♯m
39
C♯m F♯m E B
43
E C♯m F♯m

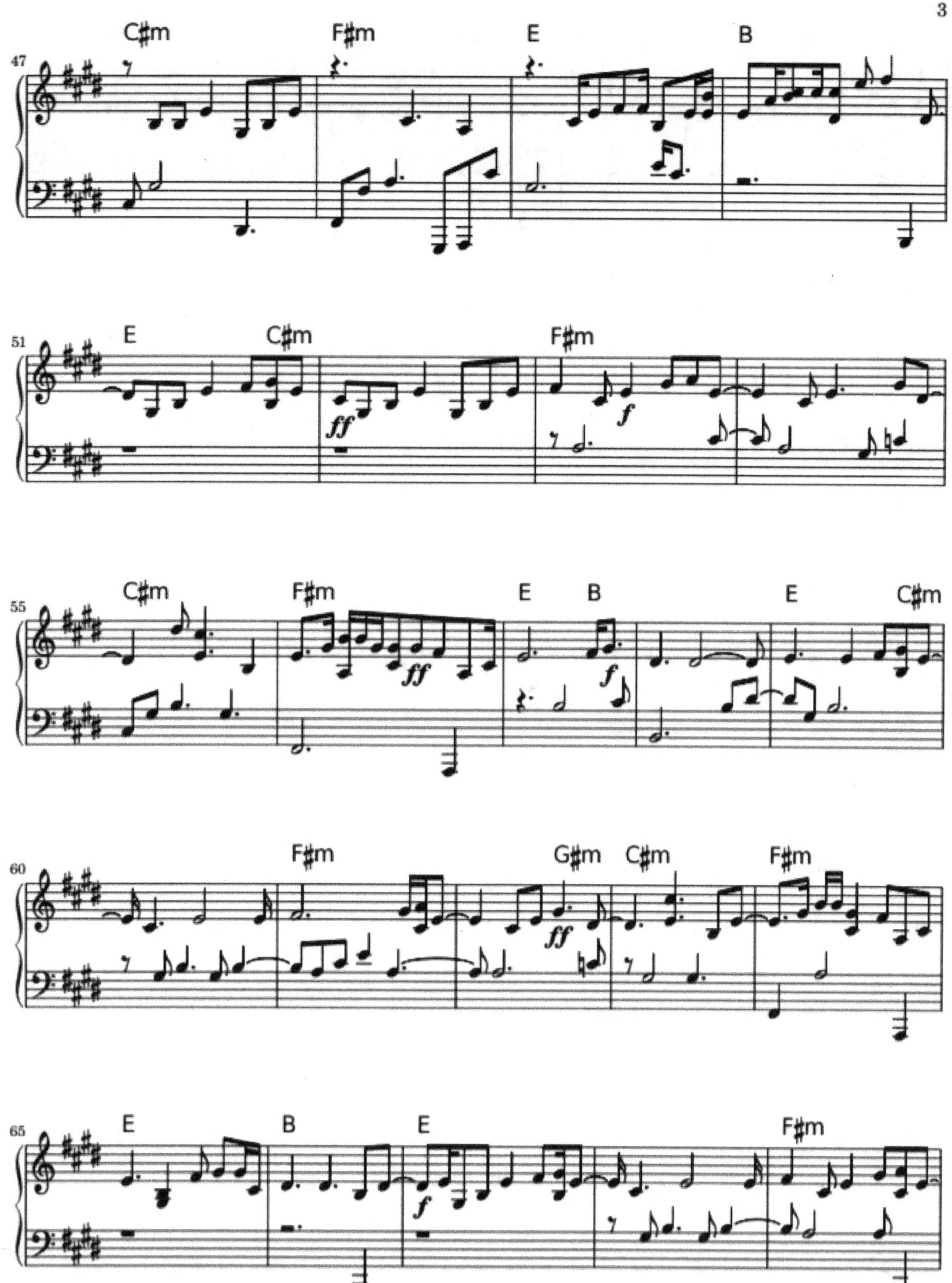

3
47
C♯m F♯m E B
51
E C♯m F♯m
ff
f
55
C♯m F♯m E B E C♯m
ff
f
60
F♯m G♯m C♯m F♯m
ff
65
E B E F♯m
f

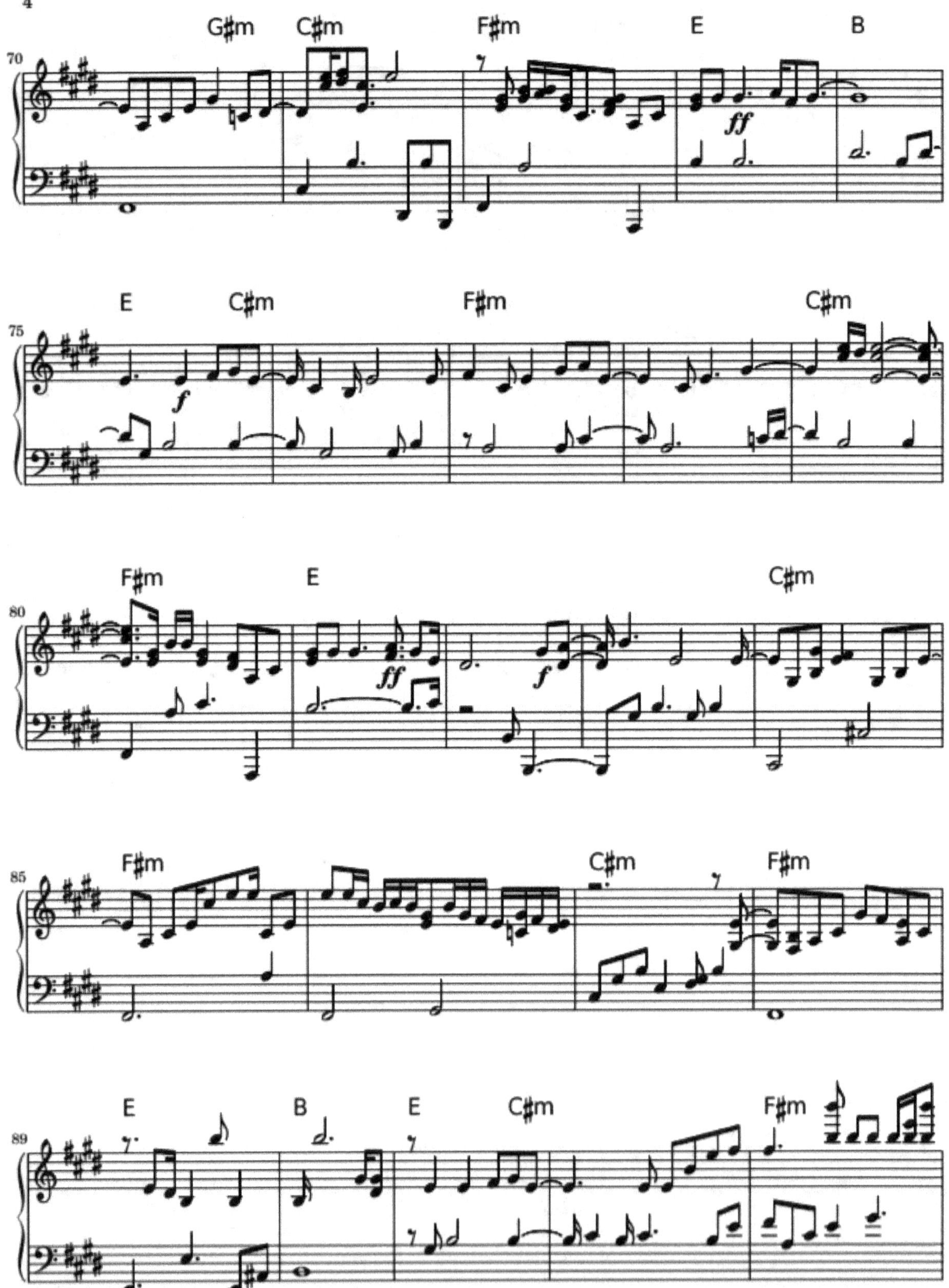
4
G♯m
C♯m
F♯m
E
B
70
ff
E
C♯m
F♯m
C♯m
75
f
F♯m
E
C♯m
80
ff
f
F♯m
C♯m
F♯m
85
E
B
E
C♯m
F♯m
89

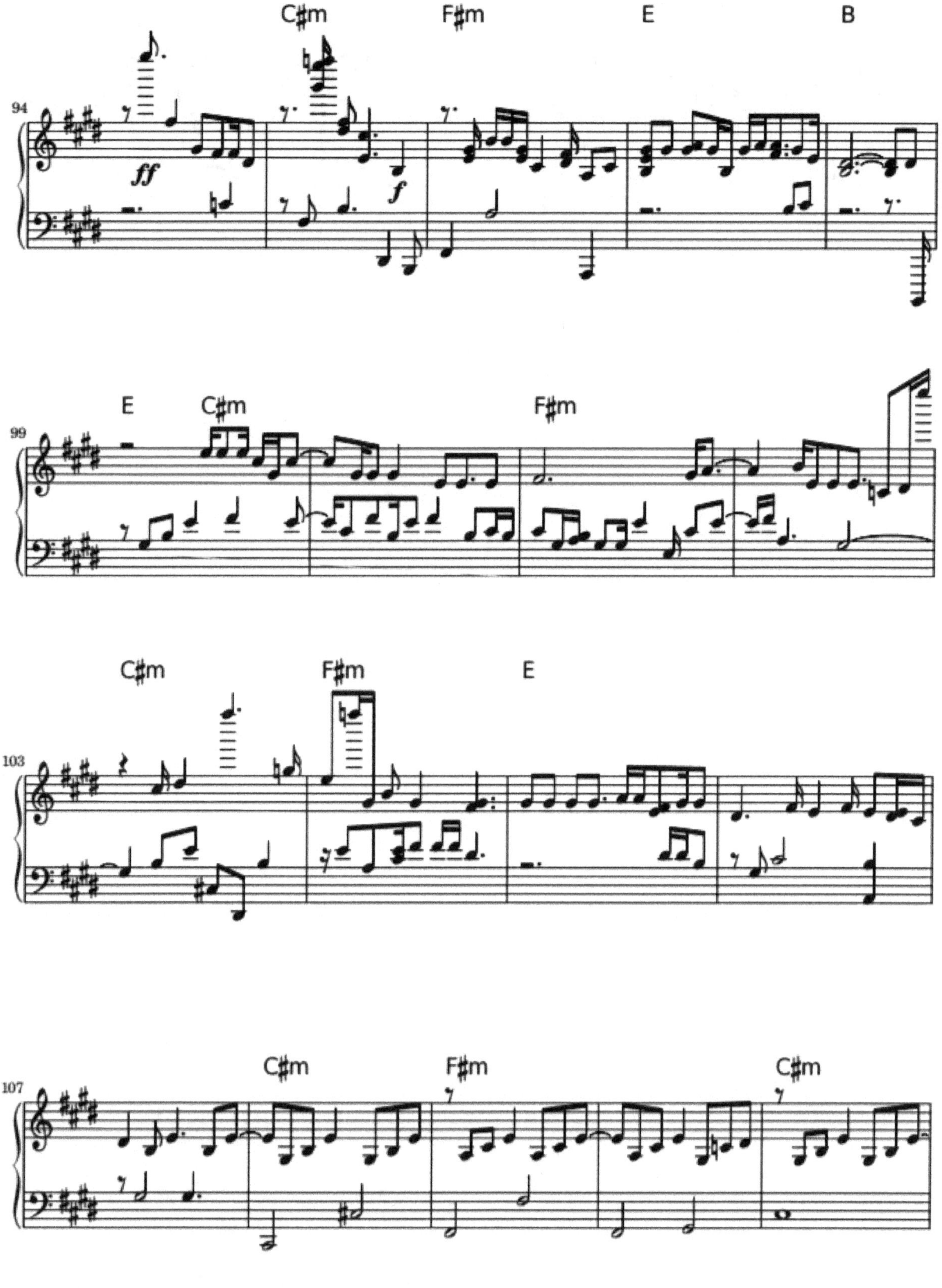

94 C♯m F♯m E B

ff *f*

99 E C♯m F♯m

103 C♯m F♯m E

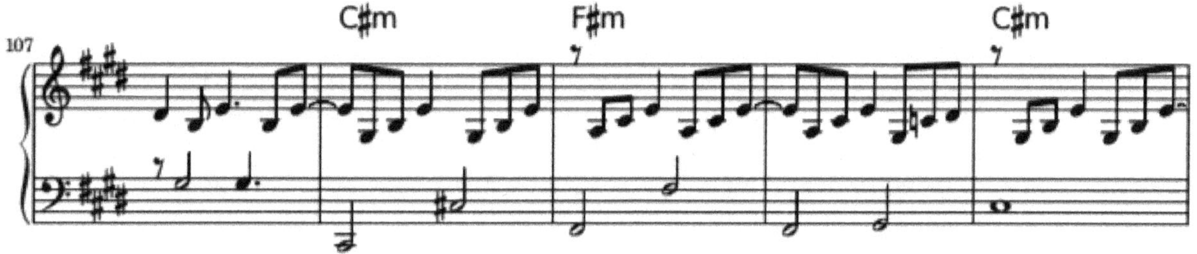

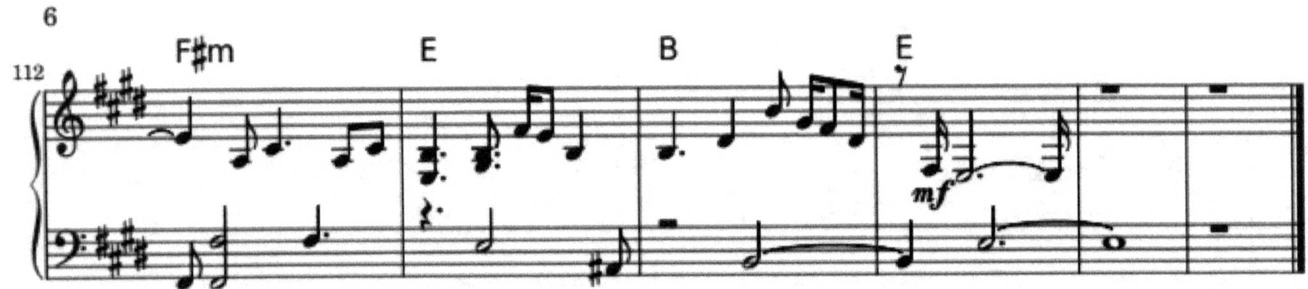
6
112
F♯m
E
B
E
mf

"I'M STILL IN LOVE"

Acoustic Grand Piano

The energetic *I'm Still in Love* is the third release from the Cat Ellington song catalog. The powerful track was written by Cat Ellington and performed by Minneapolis native Jaki Cavins for *Dual Mania (The Original Motion Picture Soundtrack)*. The track was co-produced by Cat Ellington and Princeton Brown for Vital Vision Records.

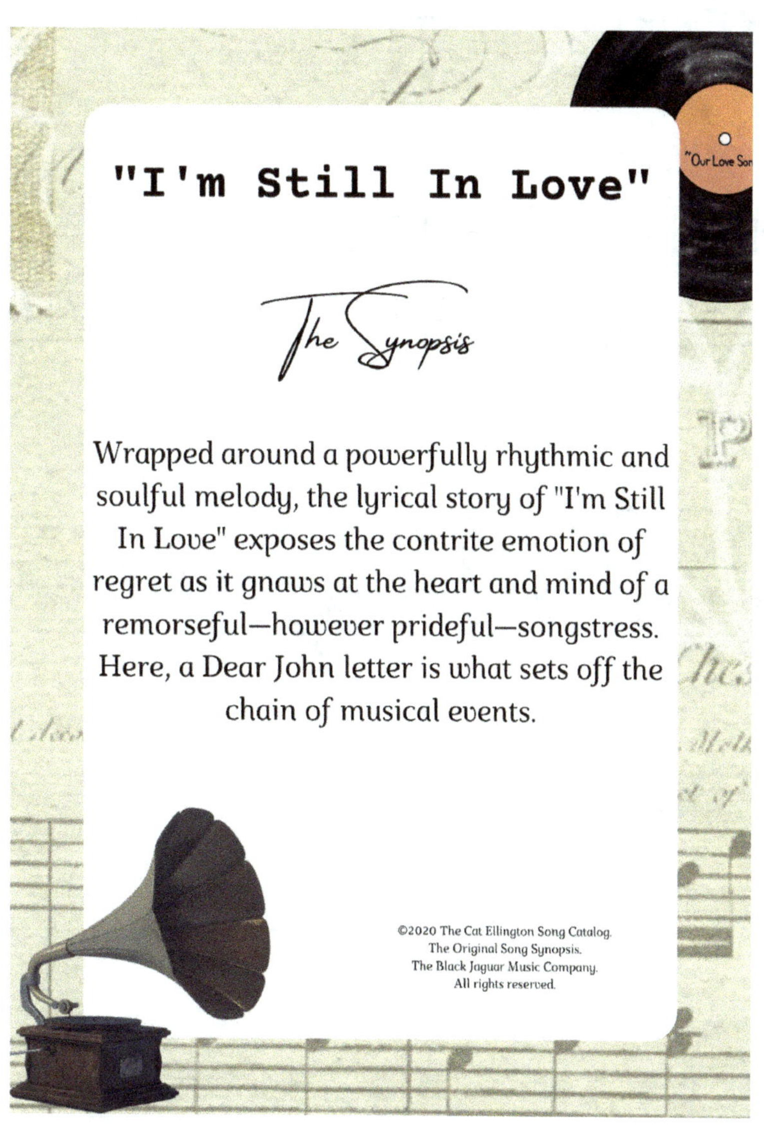

I'M STILL IN LOVE (Acoustic Grand Piano)

Composers: Cat Ellington / Princeton Brown

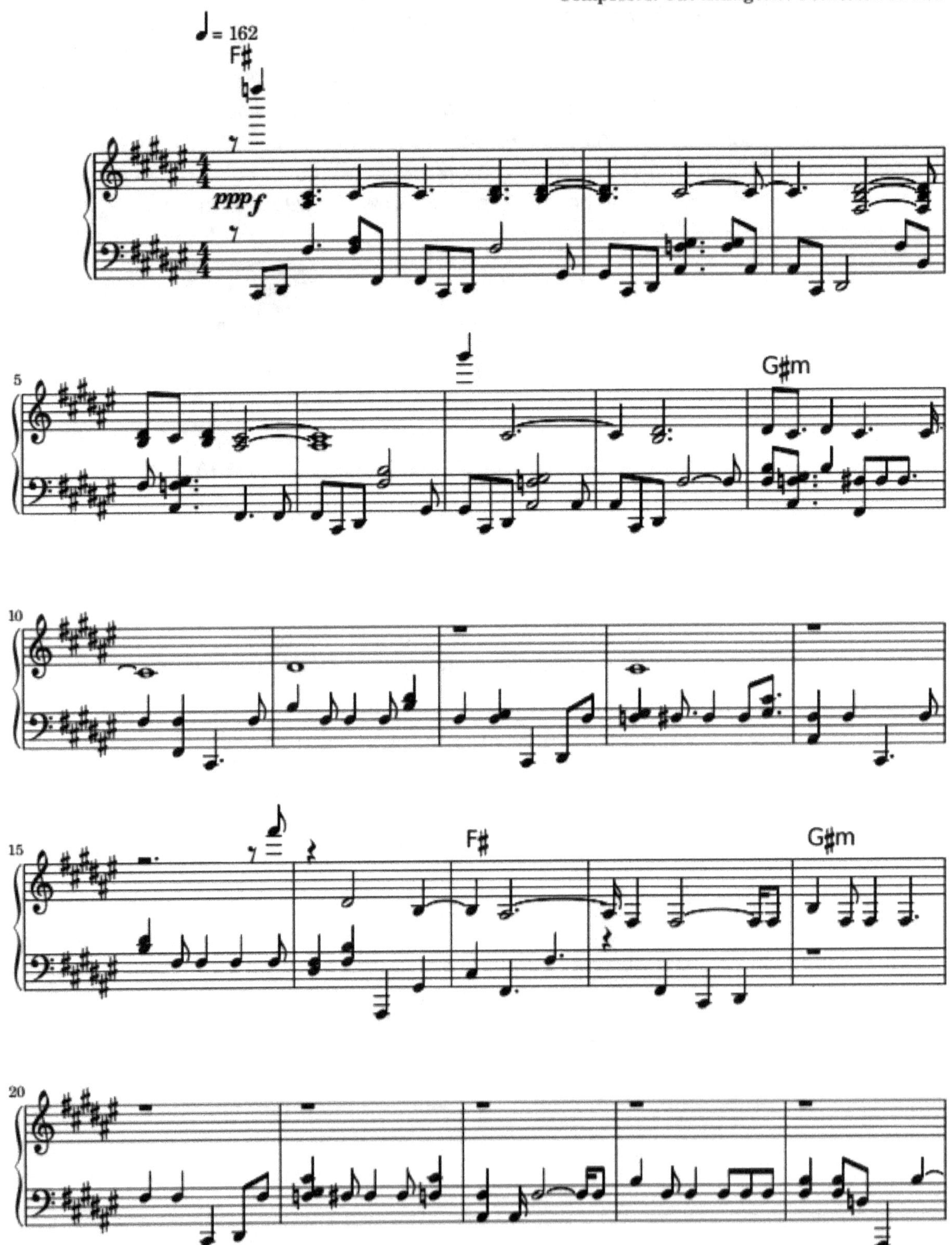

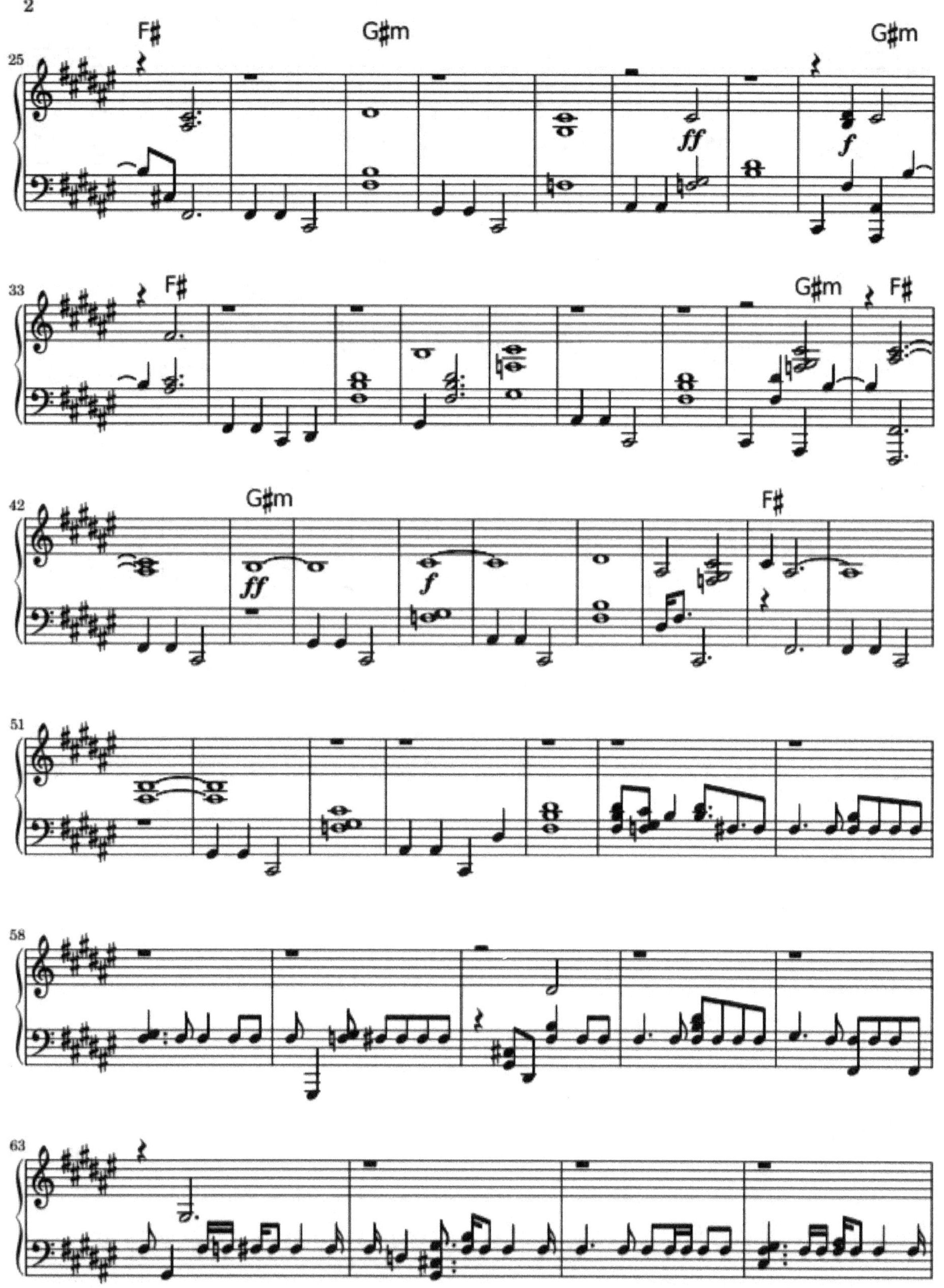
2
F♯
G♯m
ff
f
G♯m
F♯
G♯m
F♯
G♯m
ff
f
F♯

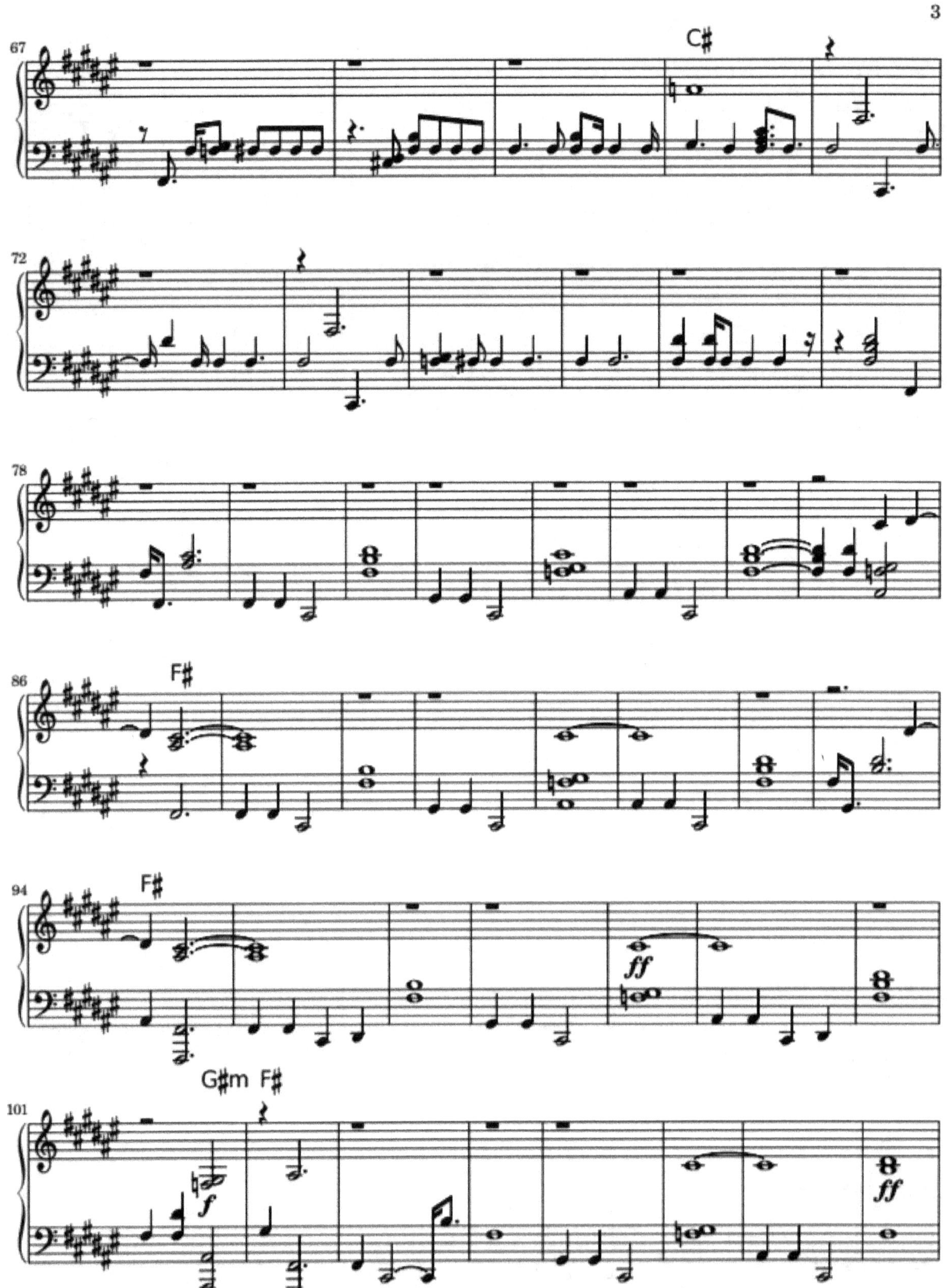
67
C♯
72
78
86
F♯
94
F♯
ff
101
G♯m F♯
f
ff

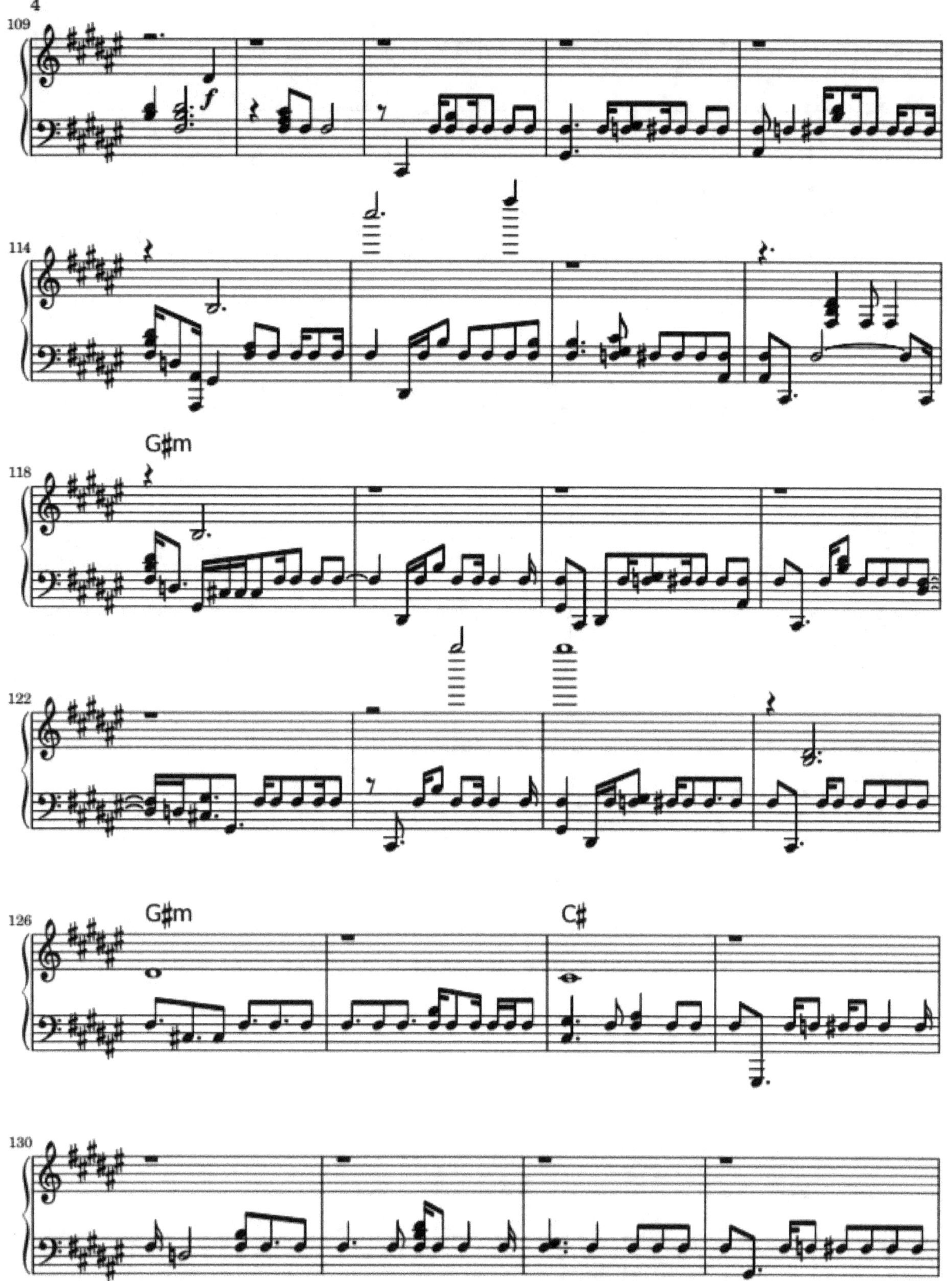
4
109
114
G♯m
118
122
G♯m
C♯
126
130

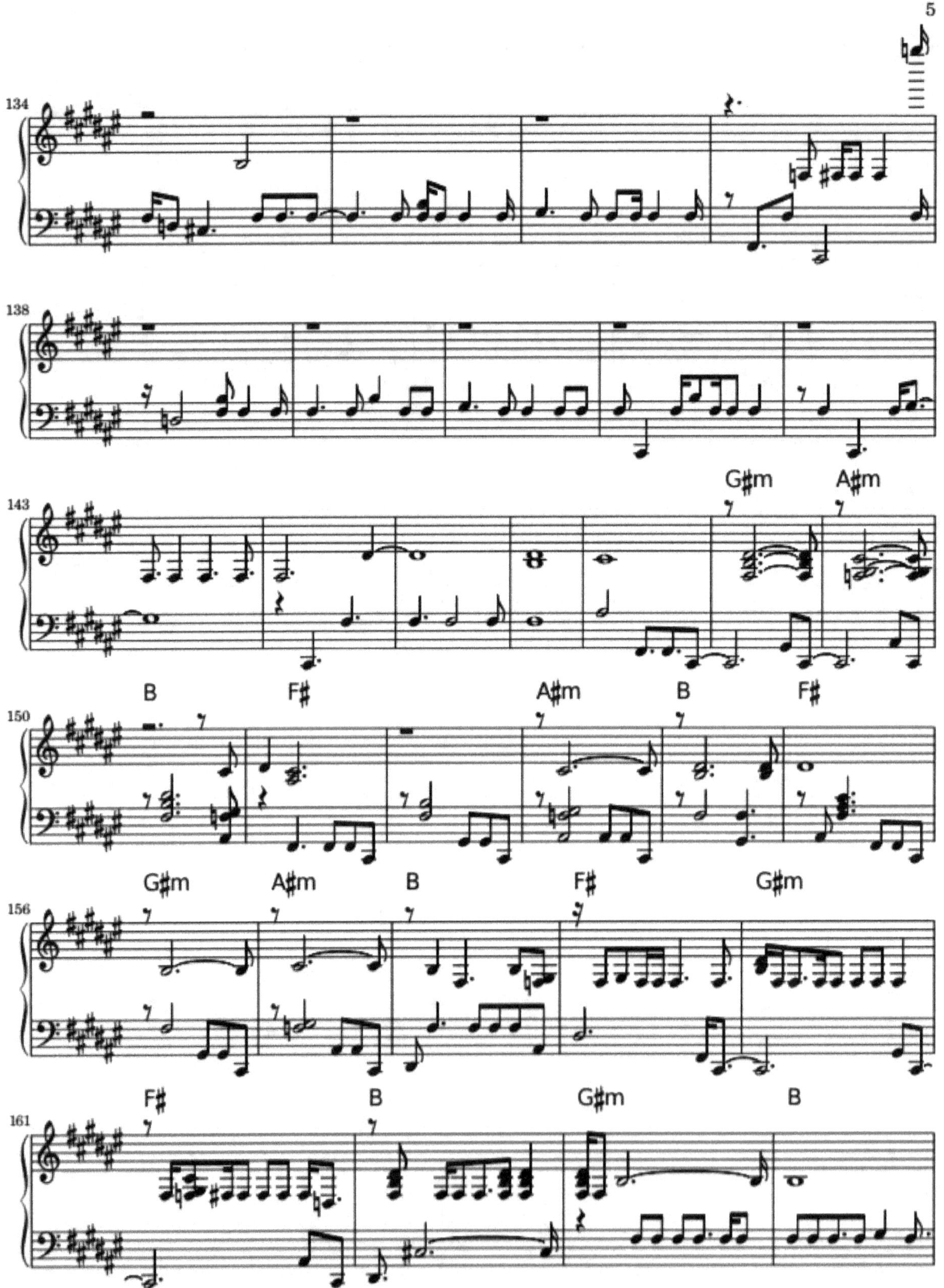
5
134
138
143
G♯m
A♯m
B
F♯
A♯m
B
F♯
150
G♯m
A♯m
B
F♯
G♯m
156
F♯
B
G♯m
B
161

6

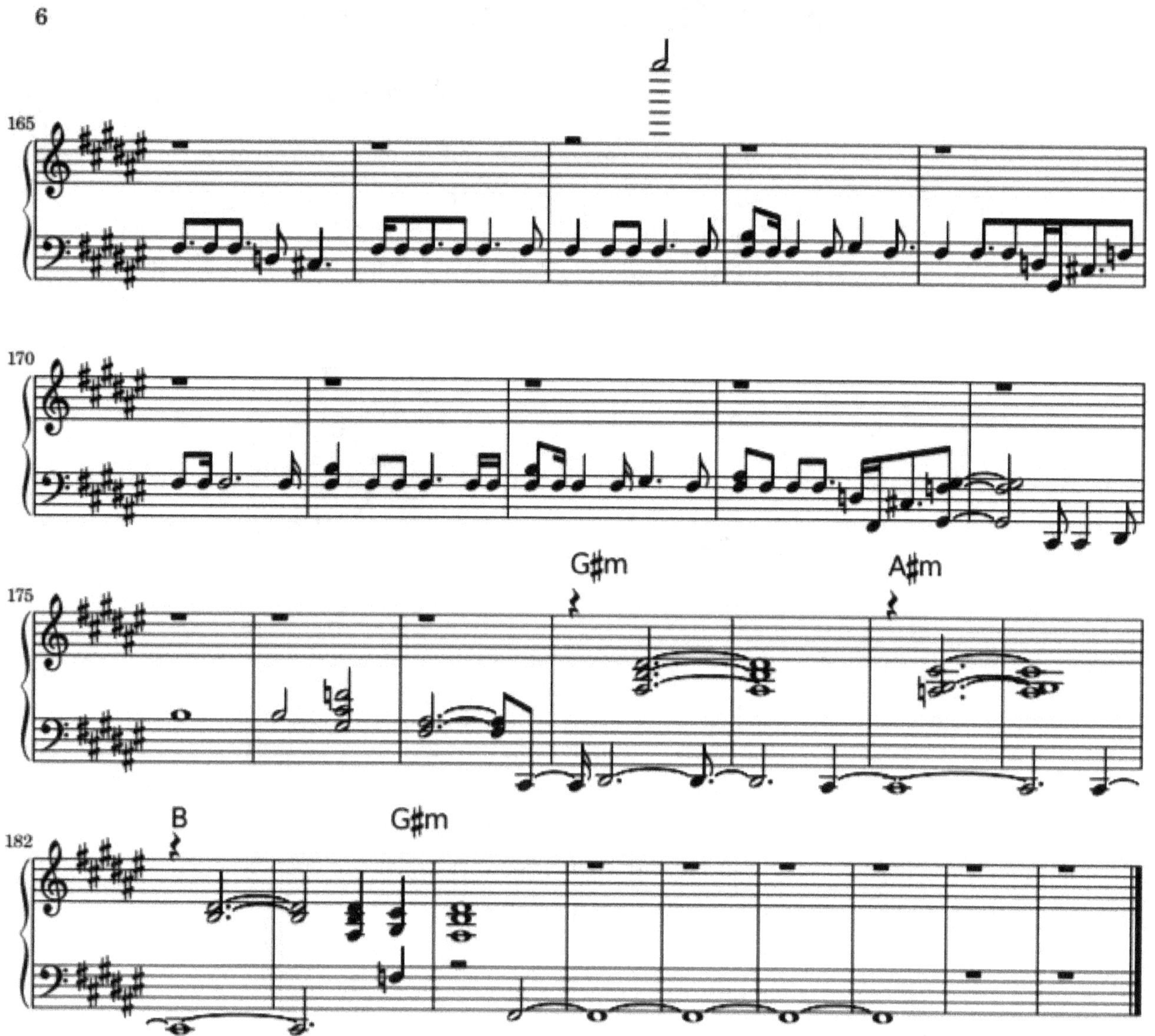

"SOMETHING IN YOUR EYES"

Acoustic Grand Piano

The jazzy *Something in Your Eyes*, the fourth release from the Cat Ellington song catalog, was written by Cat Ellington and performed by Minneapolis native Jaki Cavins for *Dual Mania (The Original Motion Picture Soundtrack)*. The track was co-produced by Cat Ellington and Princeton Brown for Vital Vision Records.

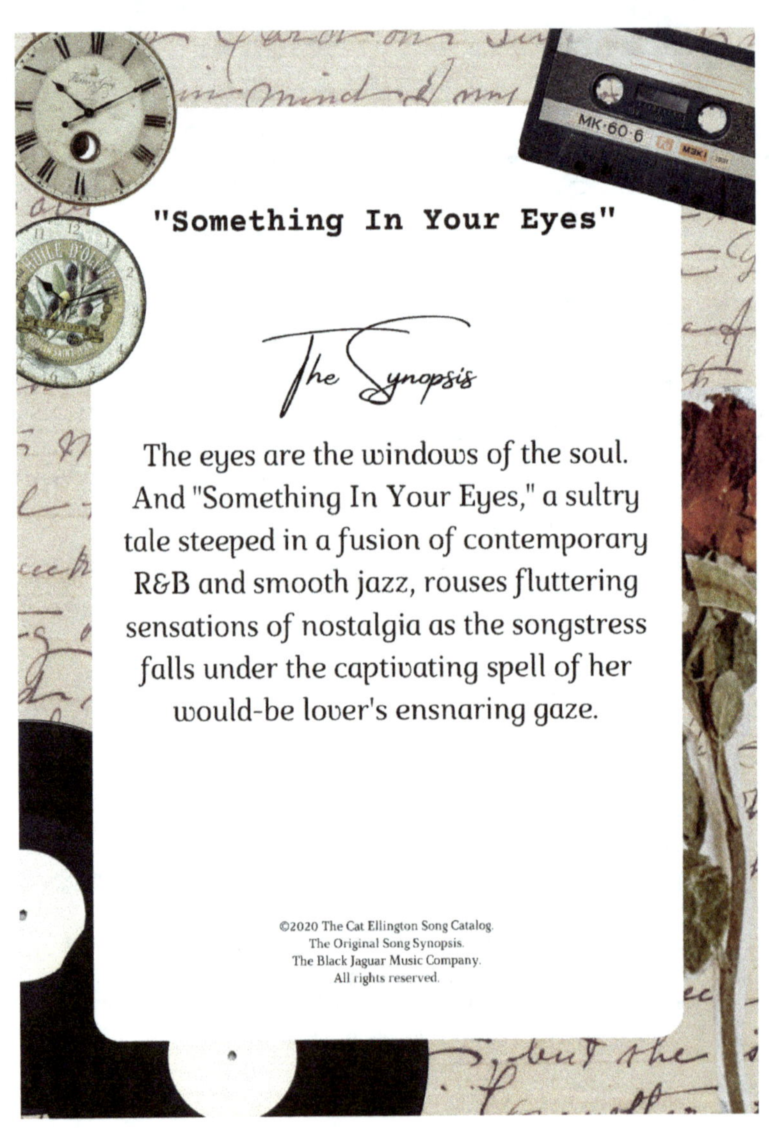

SOMETHING IN YOUR EYES (Acoustic Grand Piano)

Composers: Cat Ellington / Princeton Brown

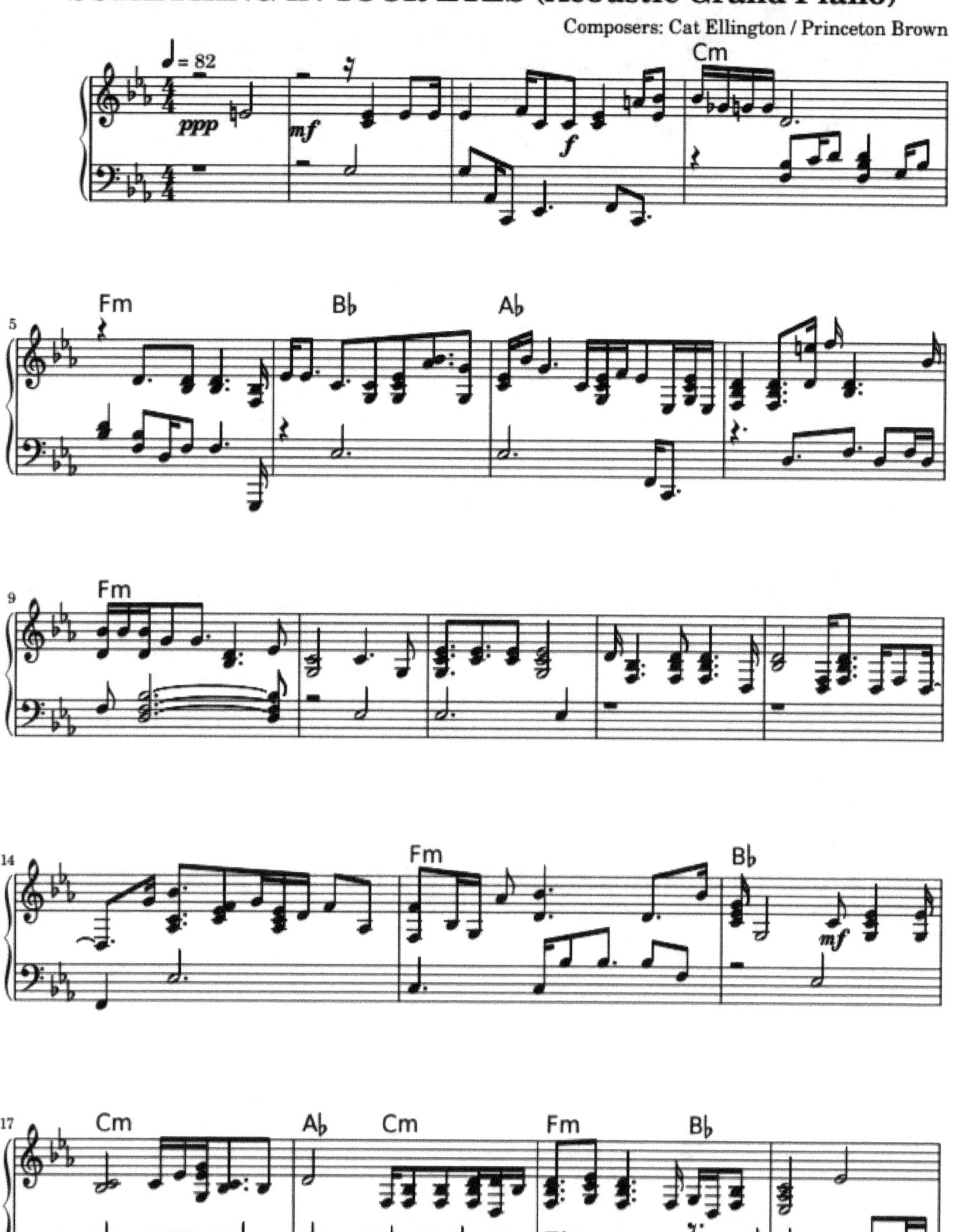

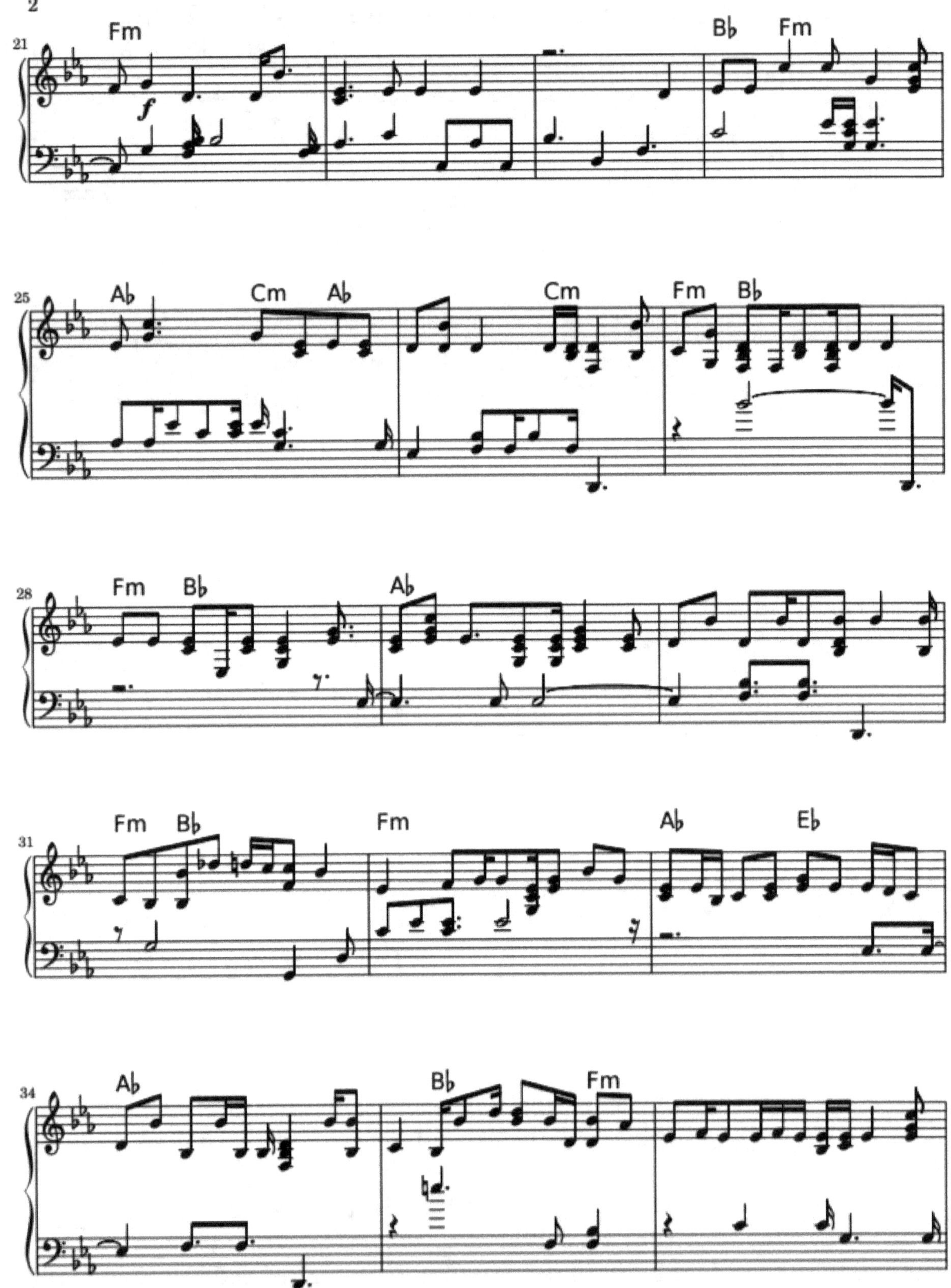
2
21 Fm Bb Fm
f
25 Ab Cm Ab Cm Fm Bb
28 Fm Bb Ab
31 Fm Bb Fm Ab Eb
34 Ab Bb Fm

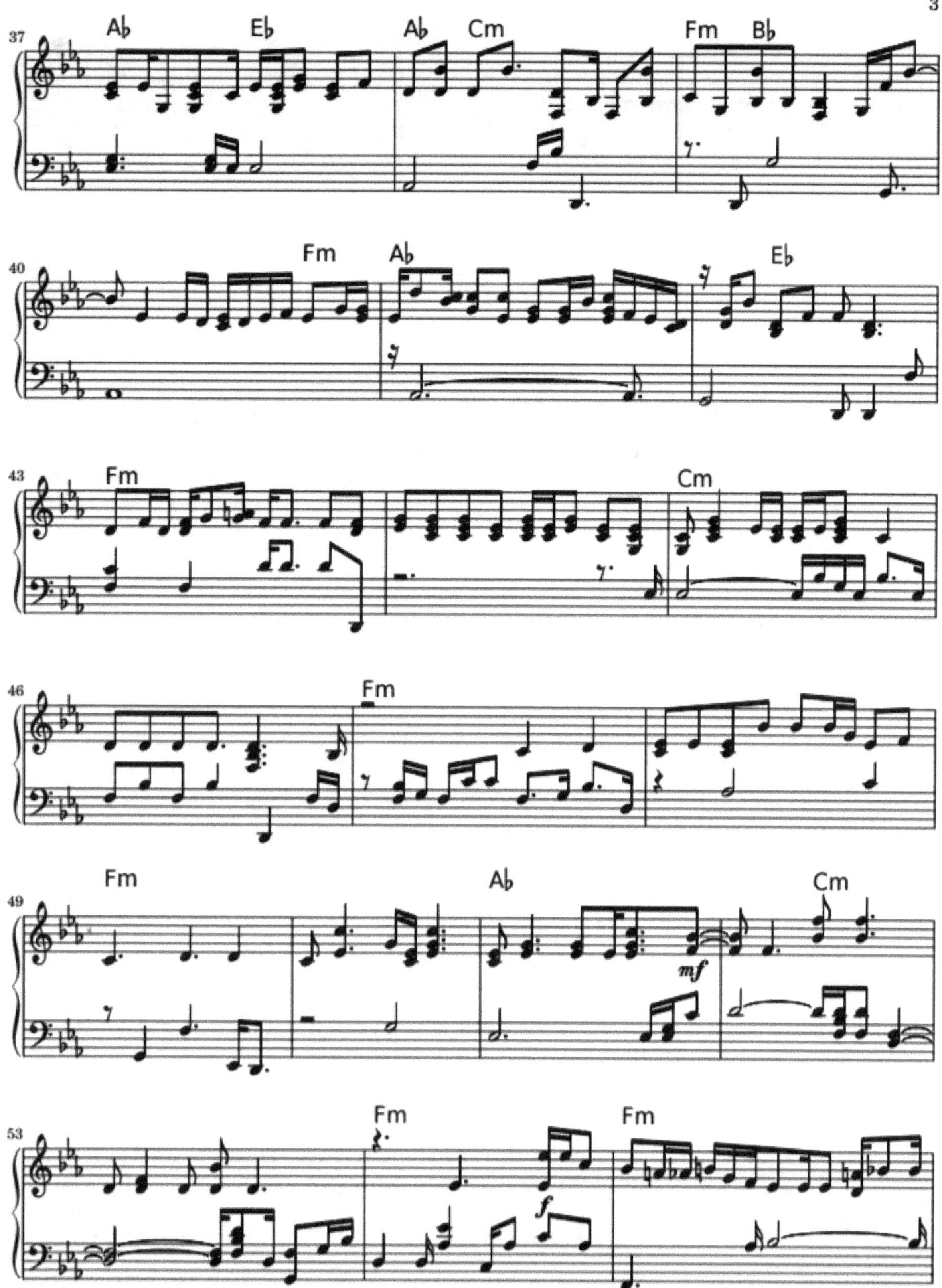
3
37
A♭
E♭
A♭
Cm
Fm
B♭
40
Fm
A♭
E♭
43
Fm
Cm
46
Fm
49
Fm
A♭
Cm
mf
53
Fm
Fm
f

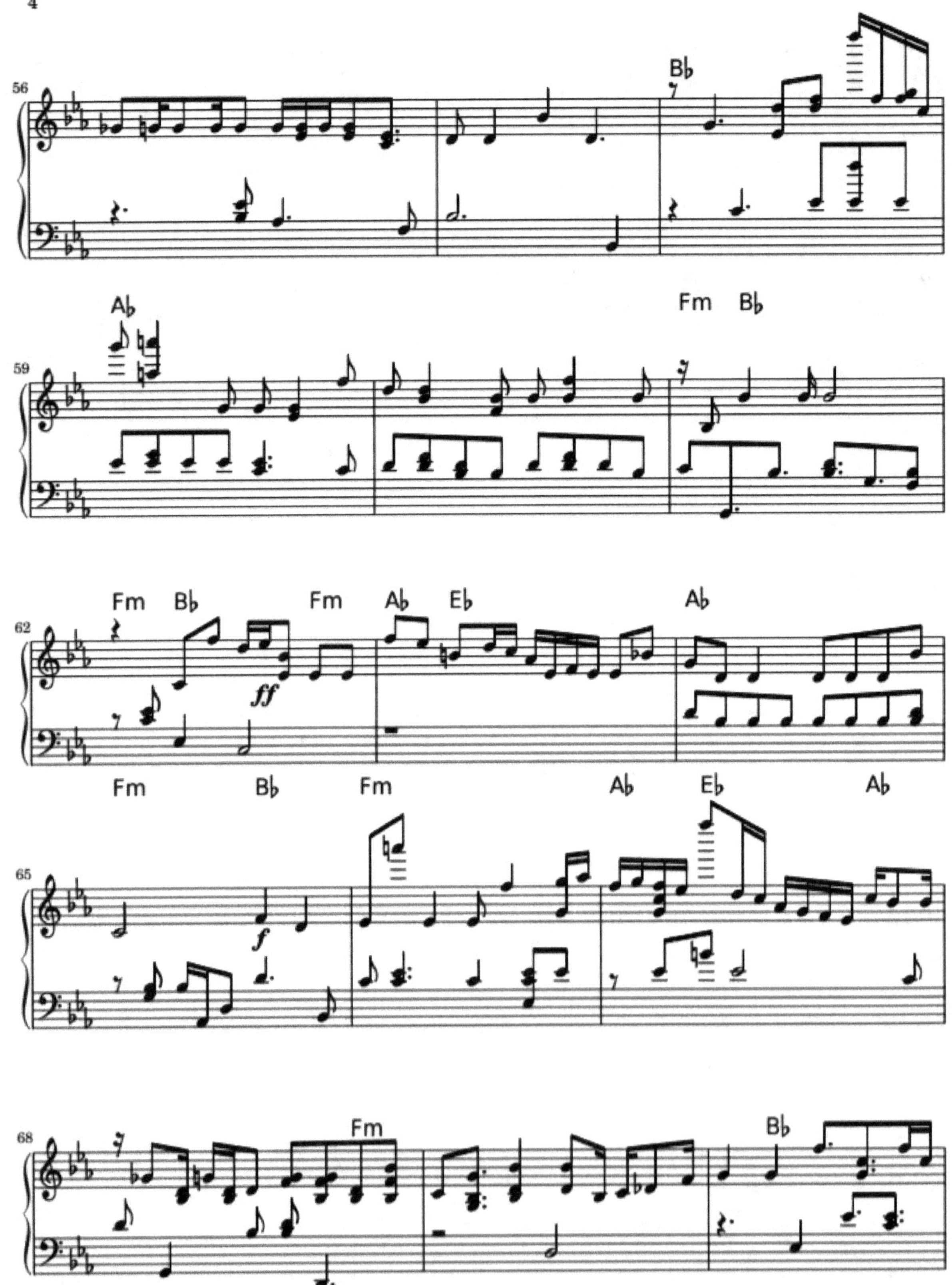
56
B♭
A♭
59
Fm B♭
Fm B♭ Fm A♭ E♭ A♭
62
ff
Fm B♭ Fm A♭ E♭ A♭
65
f
68
Fm
B♭

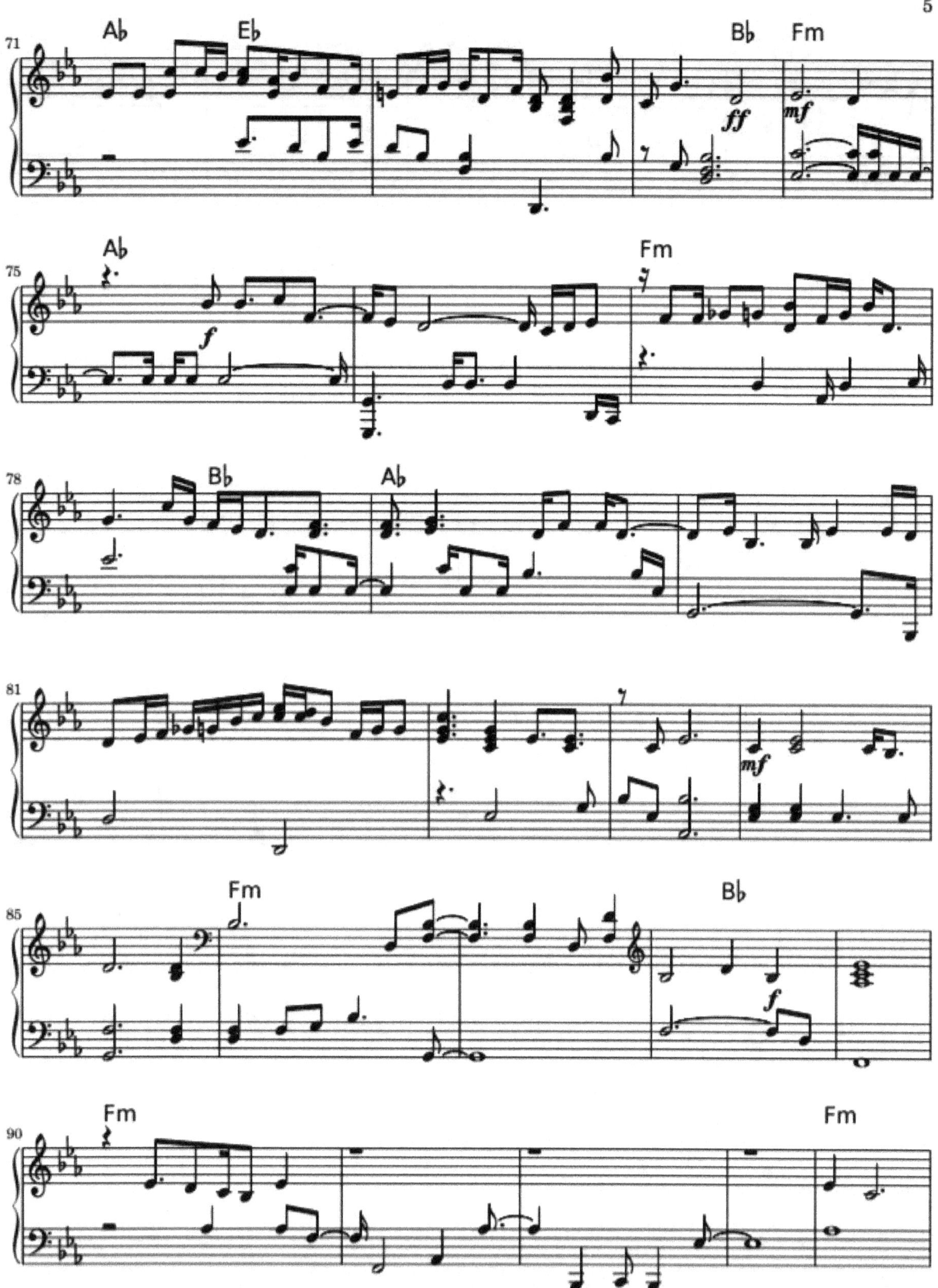
71
A♭ E♭ B♭ Fm
ff mf
75
A♭ Fm
f
78
B♭ A♭
81
mf
85
Fm B♭
f
90
Fm Fm

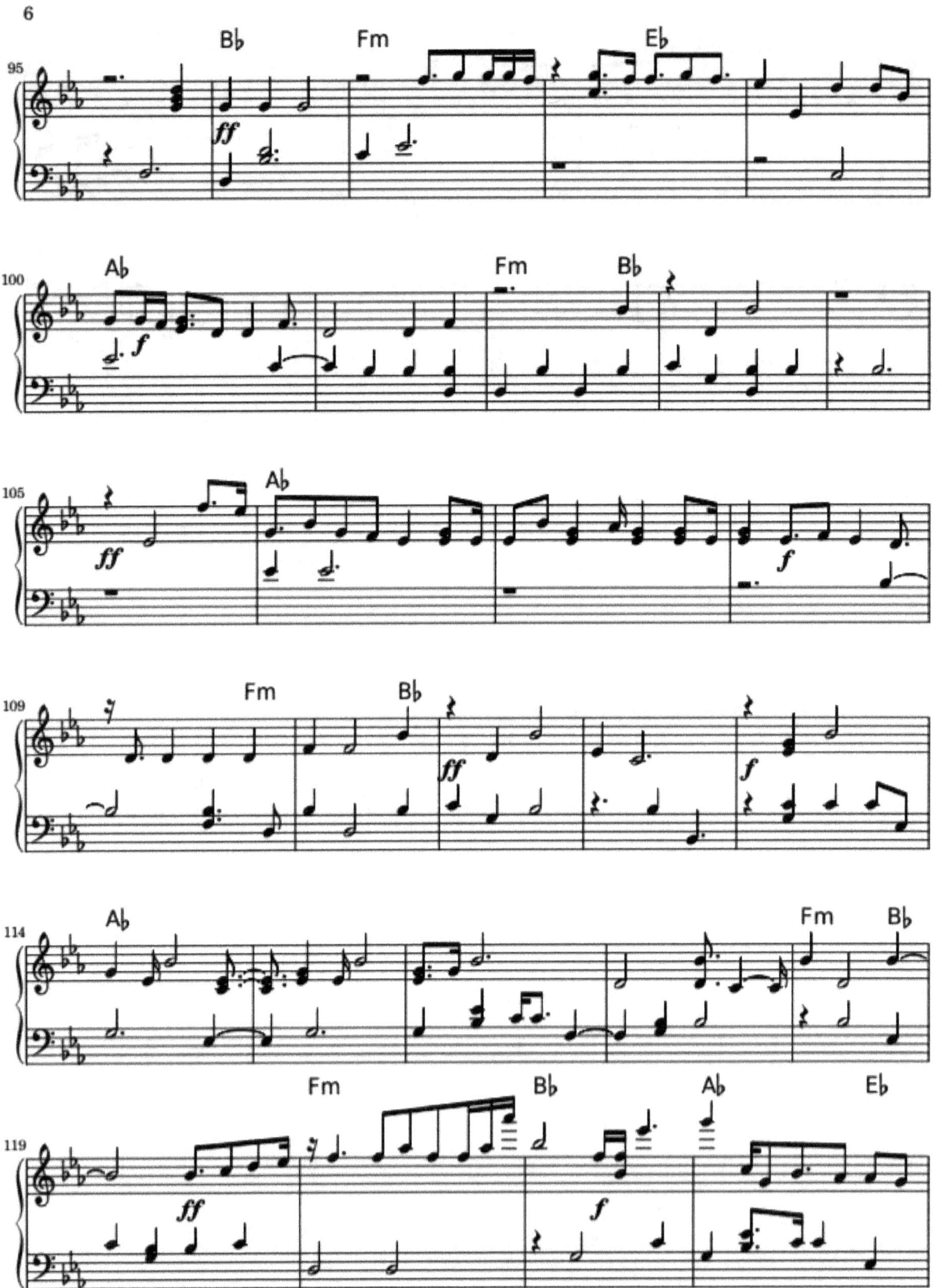
6
95
B♭
Fm
E♭
ff
100
A♭
f
Fm
B♭
105
ff
A♭
f
109
Fm
B♭
ff
f
114
A♭
Fm
B♭
119
Fm
B♭
A♭
E♭
ff
f

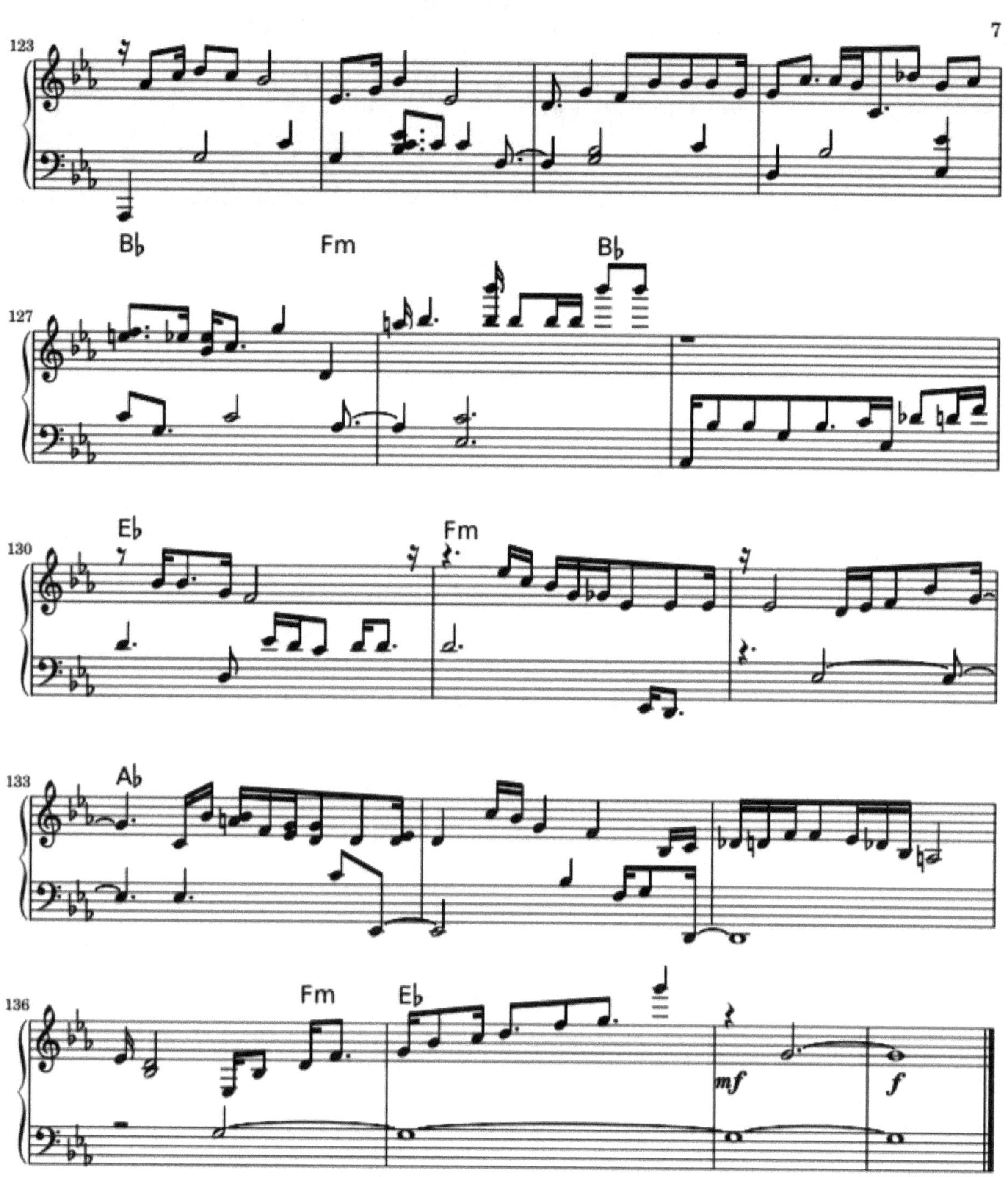
123
7
B♭
Fm
B♭
127
E♭
Fm
130
133
A♭
136
Fm
E♭
mf
f

"GETT OUT"

Acoustic Guitar

The heavy metal track, *Gett Out*, the fifth release from the Cat Ellington song catalog, was co-written by Cat Ellington and Joseph Strickland and performed by Minneapolis native and Hippo Campus member DeCarlo Jackson for *Dual Mania (The Original Motion Picture Soundtrack)*. The track was co-produced by Cat Ellington and Princeton Brown for Vital Vision Records.

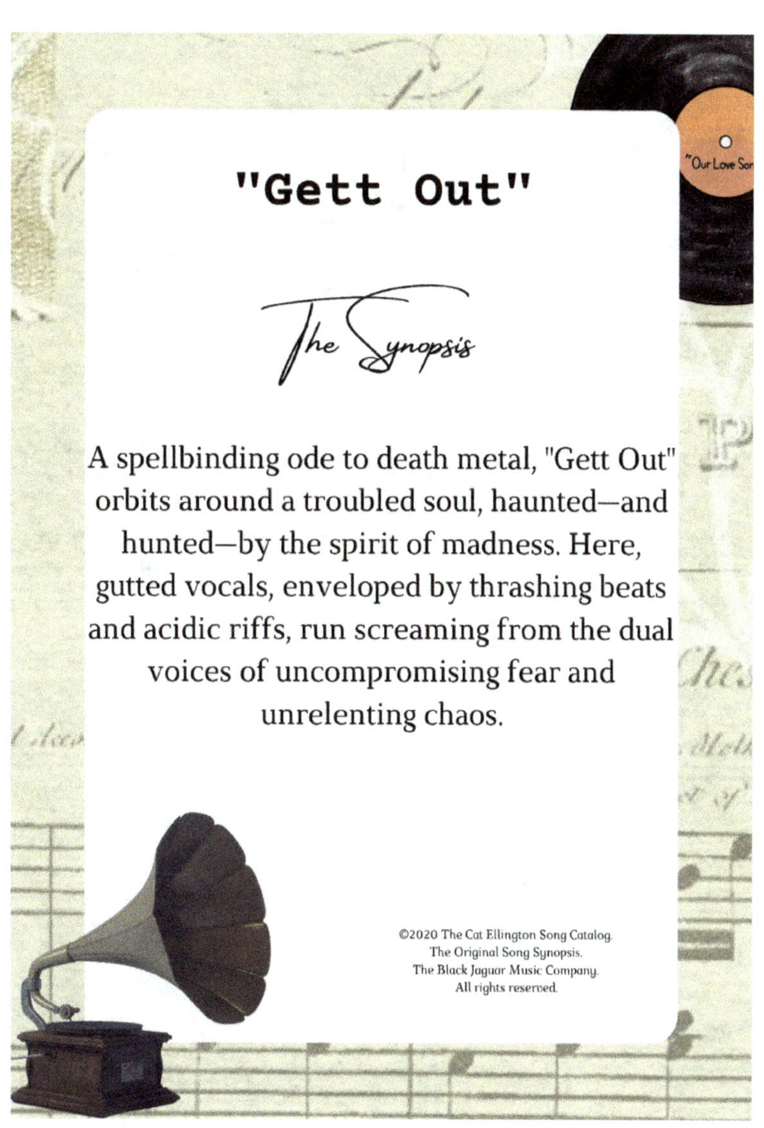

GETT OUT (Acoustic Guitar)

Composers: Cat Ellington / Joseph Strickland / Greg Schutte / Princeton Brown

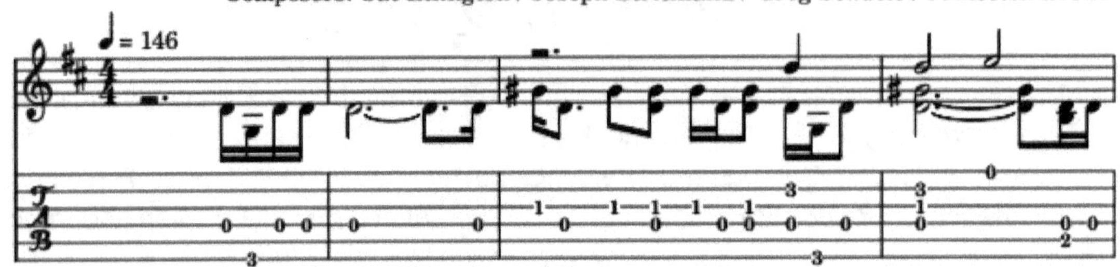

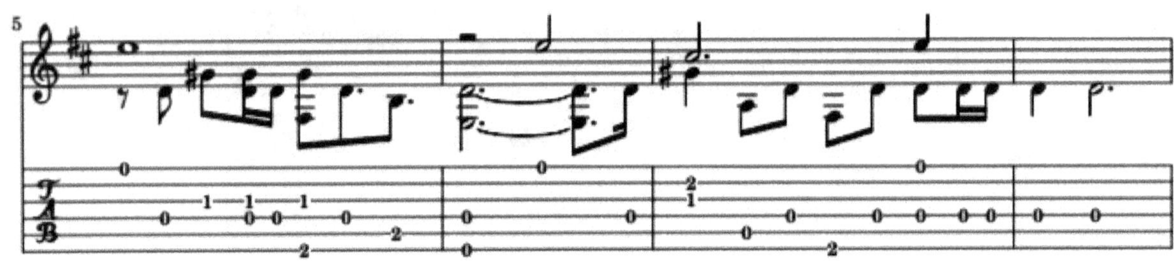

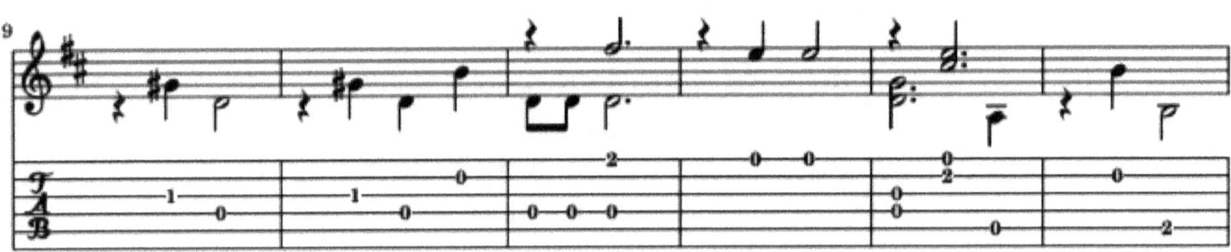

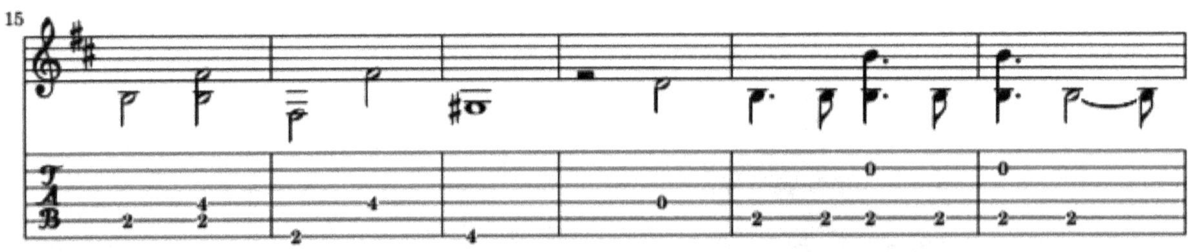

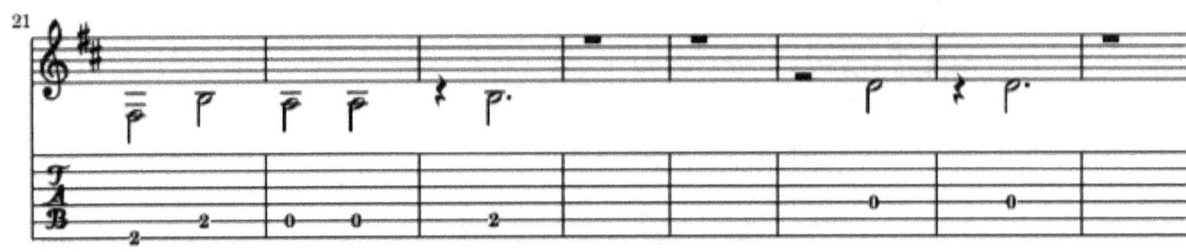

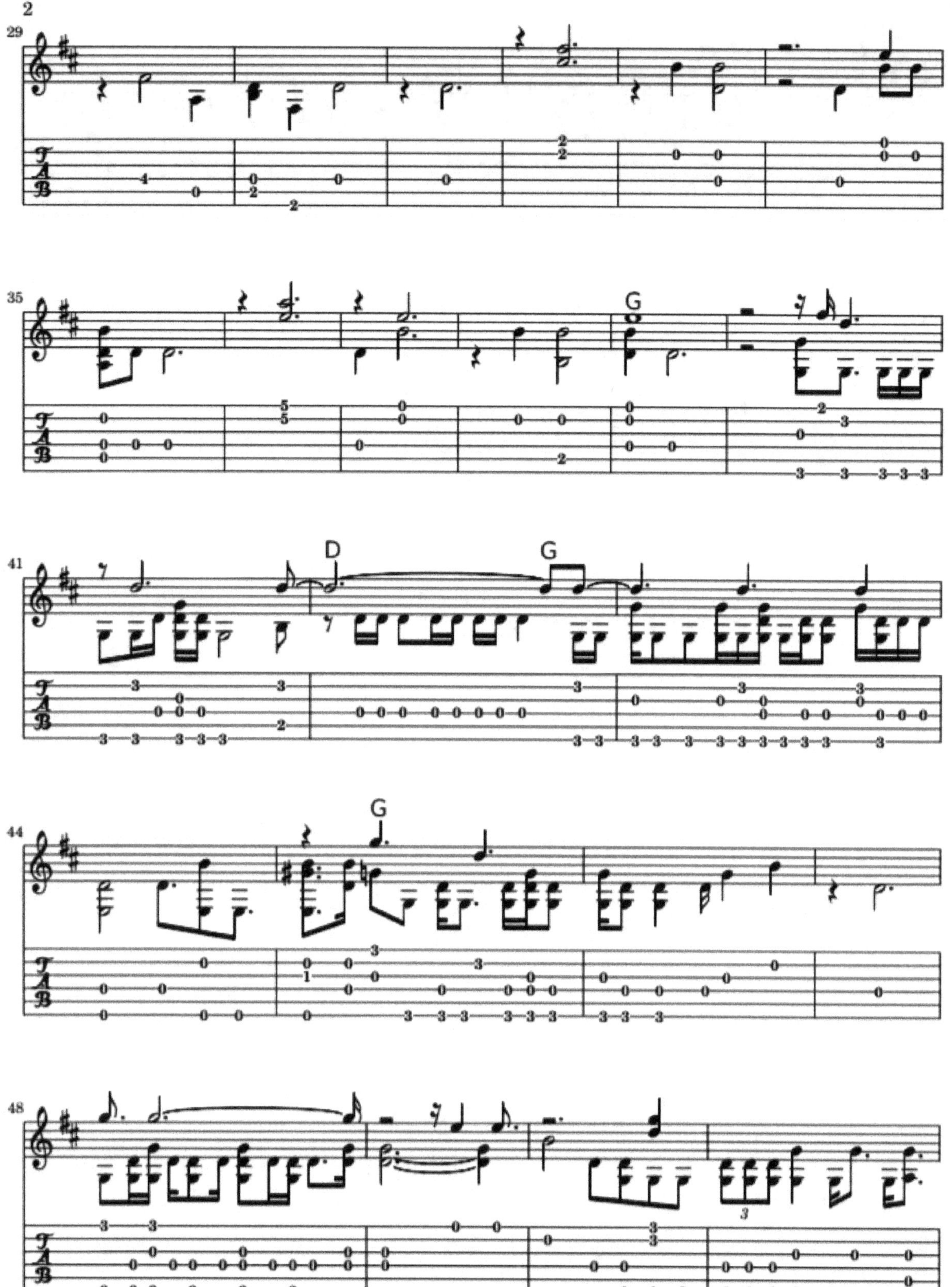
2
G
D
G
G

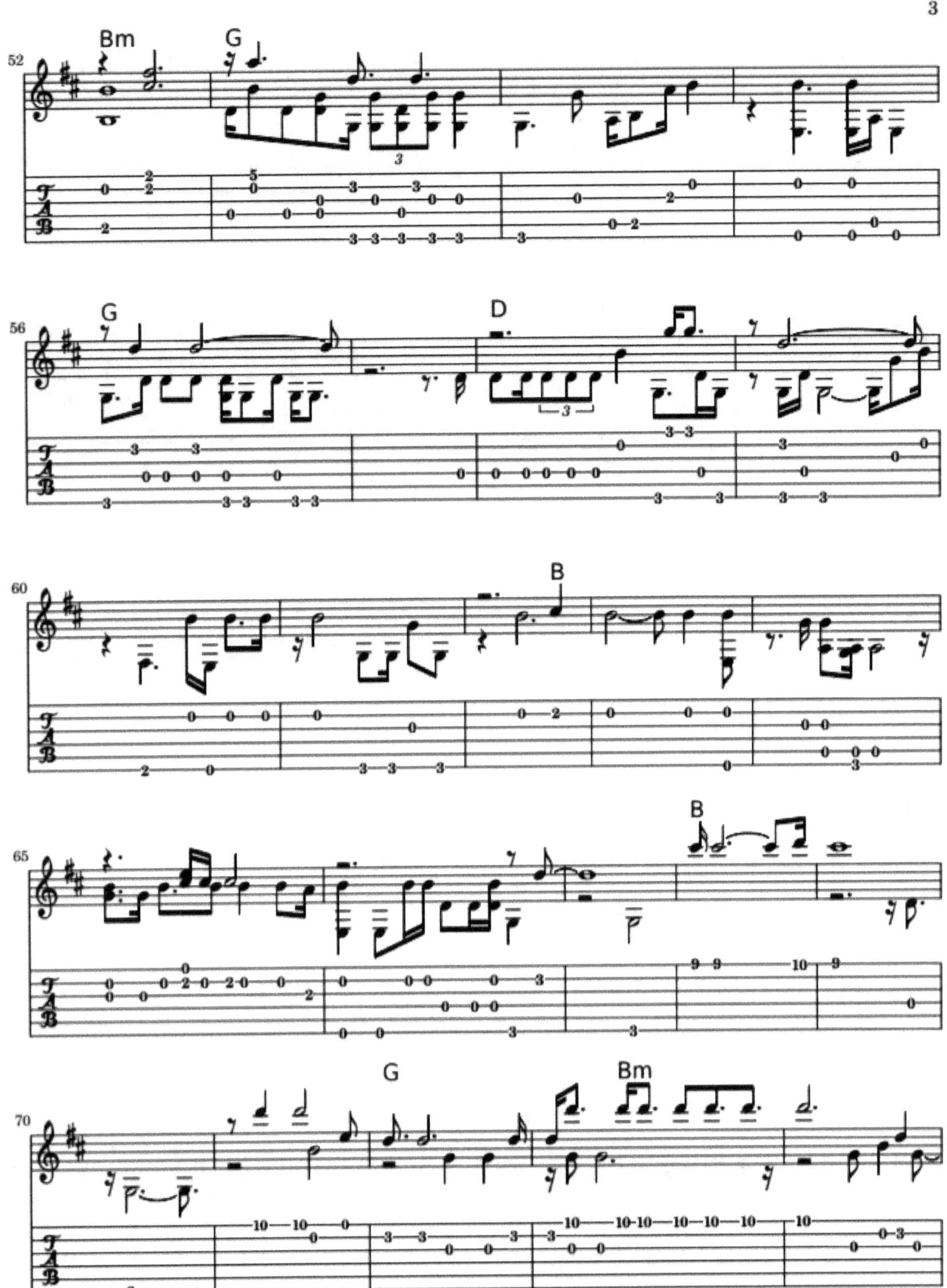
52
Bm
G
56
G
D
60
B
65
B
70
G
Bm

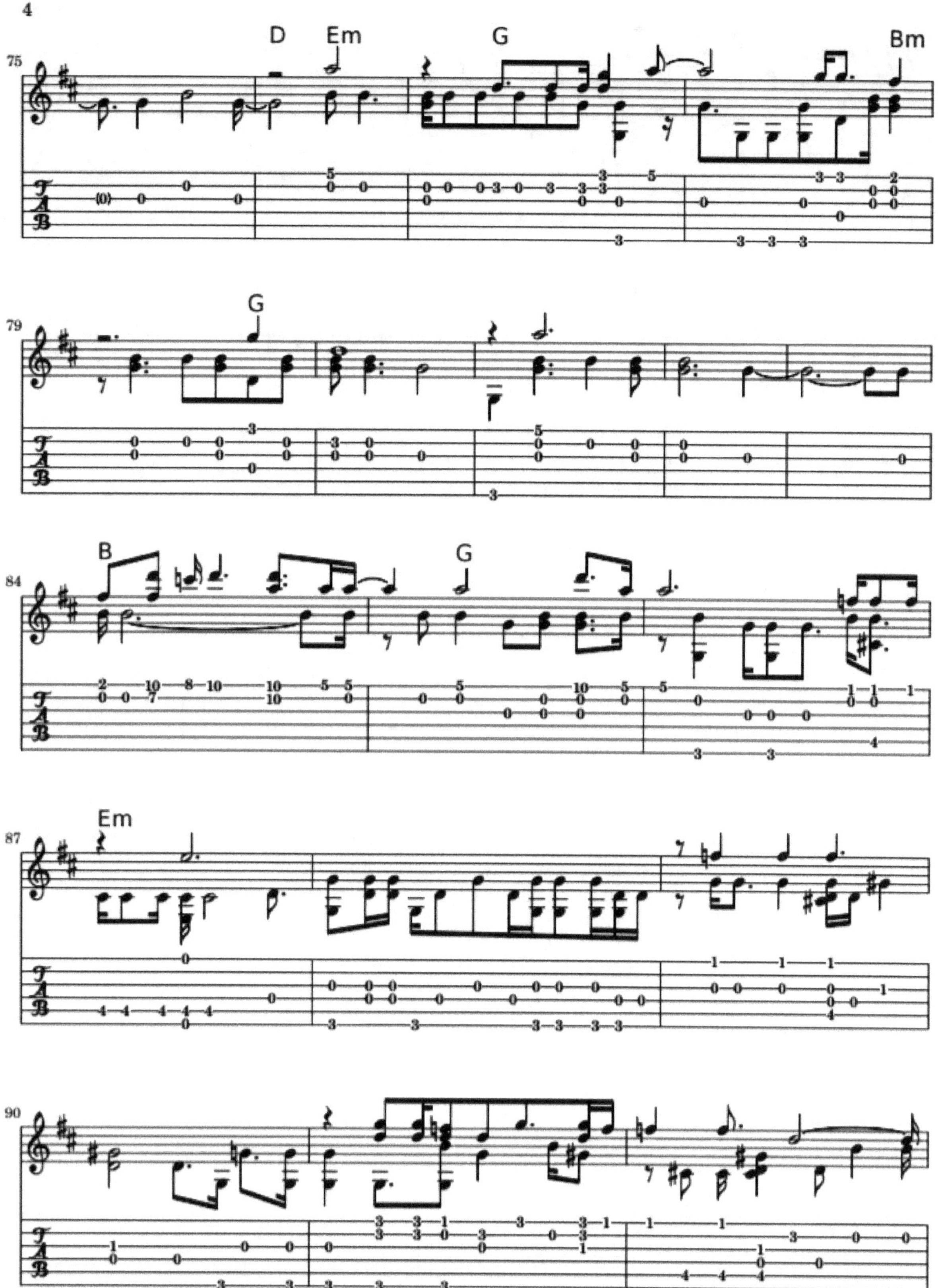
4
D
Em
G
Bm
G
B
G
Em

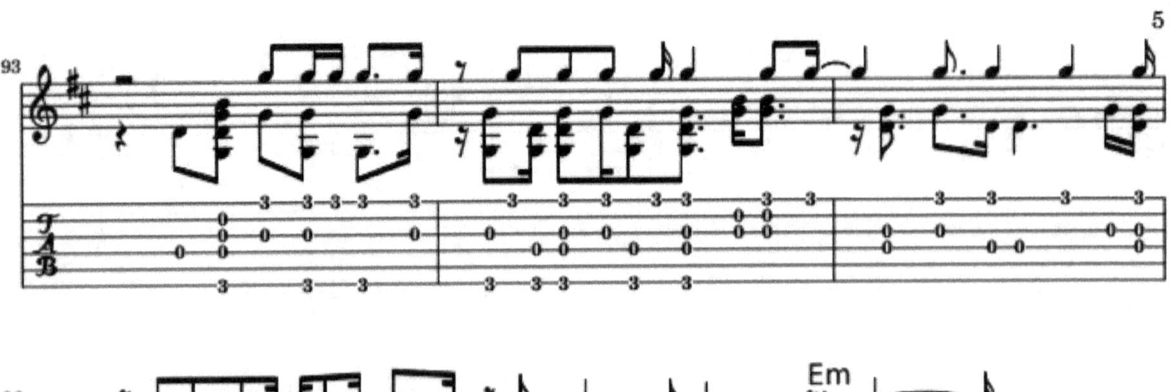
93
5

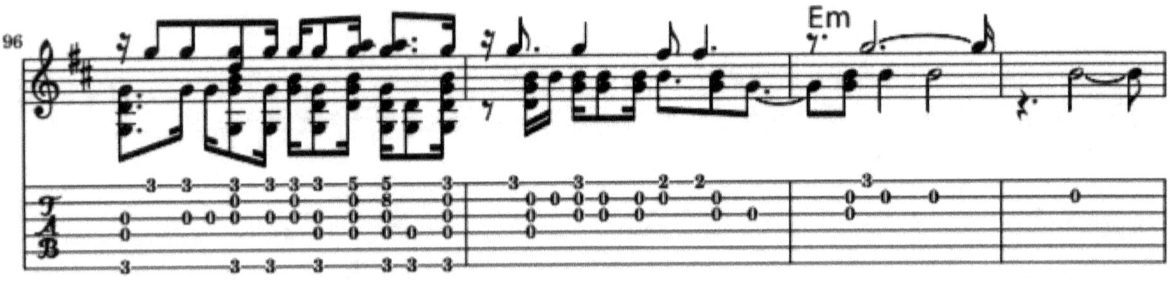
96
Em

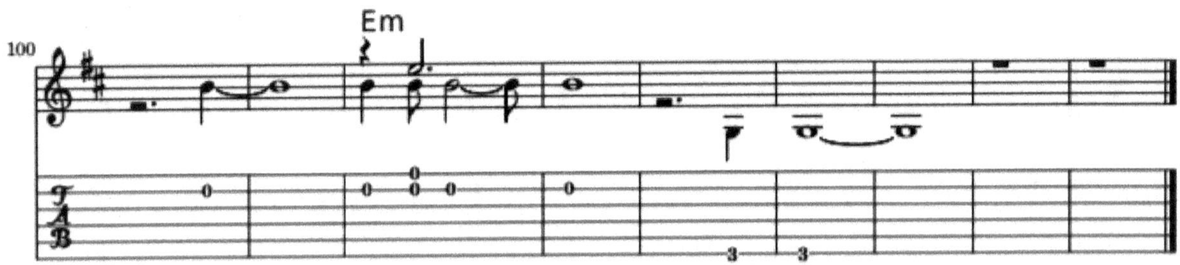
100
Em

Acknowledgments

Vital Vision Film Music would like to thank Cat Ellington, The Black Jaguar Music Company, Dark Planet Publishing, Joseph Strickland, Vital Vision Records, Greg "Big G" Schutte, Princeton Brown for Prince Marae Music, and our copyist friends at Melody Scanner Transcriptions Inc. for the print of this musical composition.

And a very special thank you to our Lord God for the exceptional gift of creativity.

THE ALBUMS...

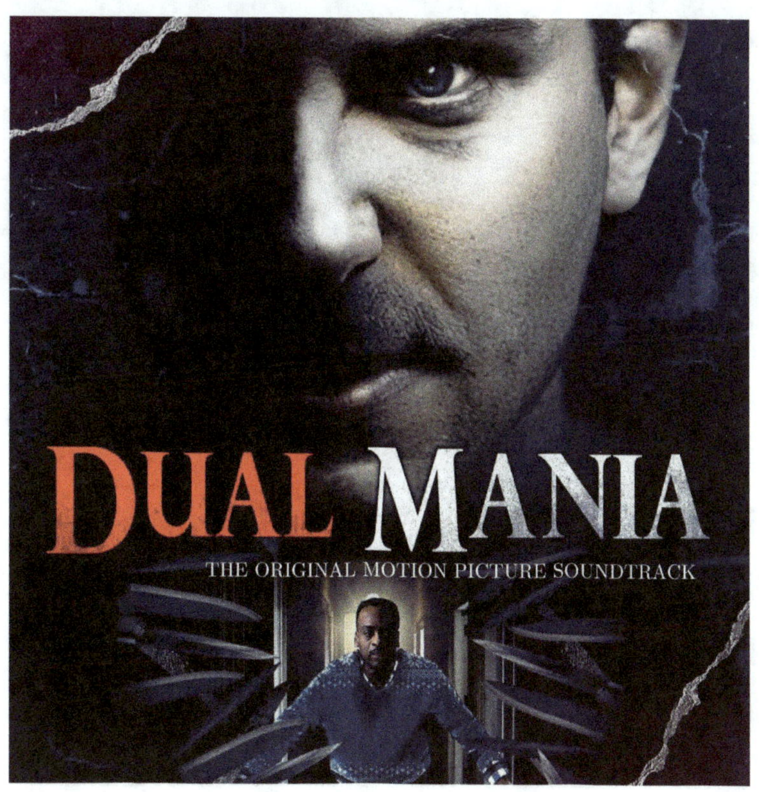

Dual Mania (The Original Motion Picture Soundtrack) (2021)
Jaki Cavins, DeCarlo Jackson, Marcus Robson
Available on Vital Vision Records
Physical album UPC code: 08521 807 6221
Digital album UPC code: 198000549985

Catalog number: VVR001

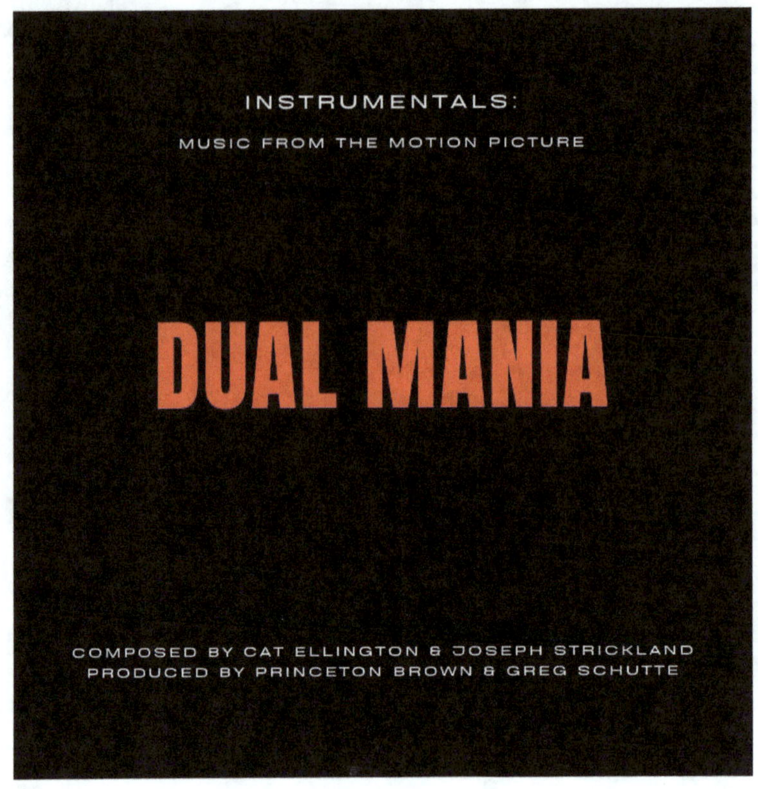

Instrumentals: Music from the Motion Picture Dual Mania (2021)
Cat Ellington, Joseph Strickland
Available on Vital Vision Records
Physical album UPC code: 08521 807 6214
Digital album UPC code: 0852118032869

Catalog number: VVR002

The Movie...

DUAL MANIA

A DANGEROUS GAME IS ABOUT TO BEGIN…

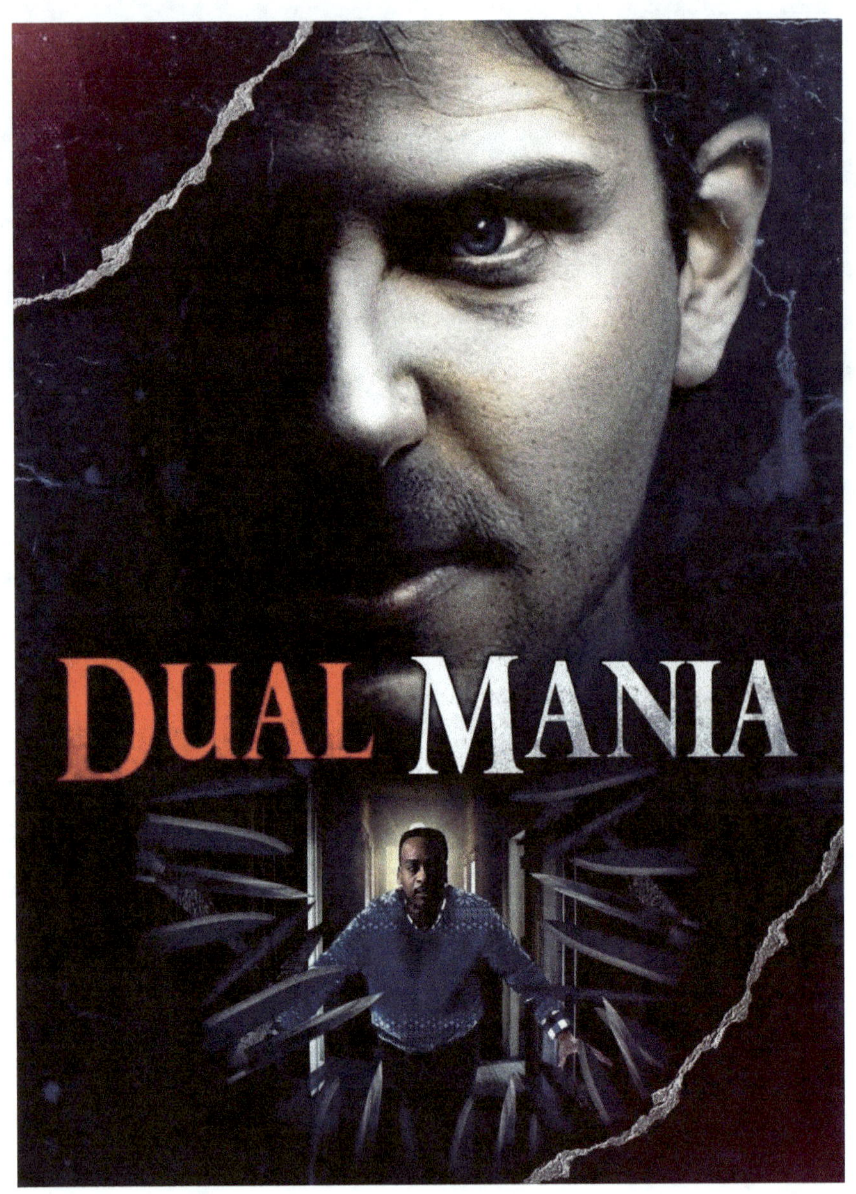

Theatrical Release / Streaming Movie Poster
Vital Vision Productions / Adler & Associates Entertainment, Inc.

Behind the Scenes...

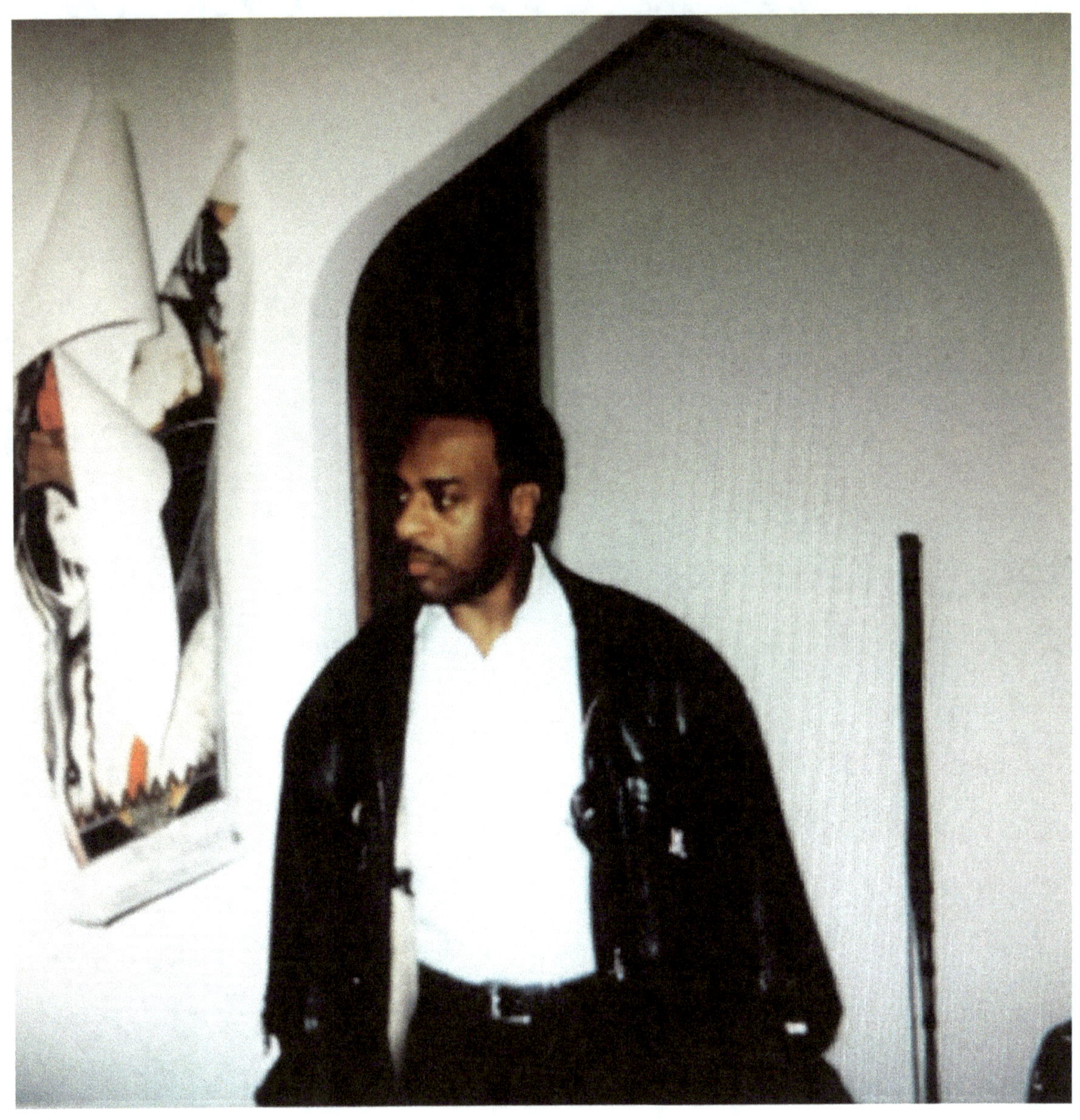

Leading man Joseph Plummer as “Dr. Steve Livingston” in “Dual Mania”

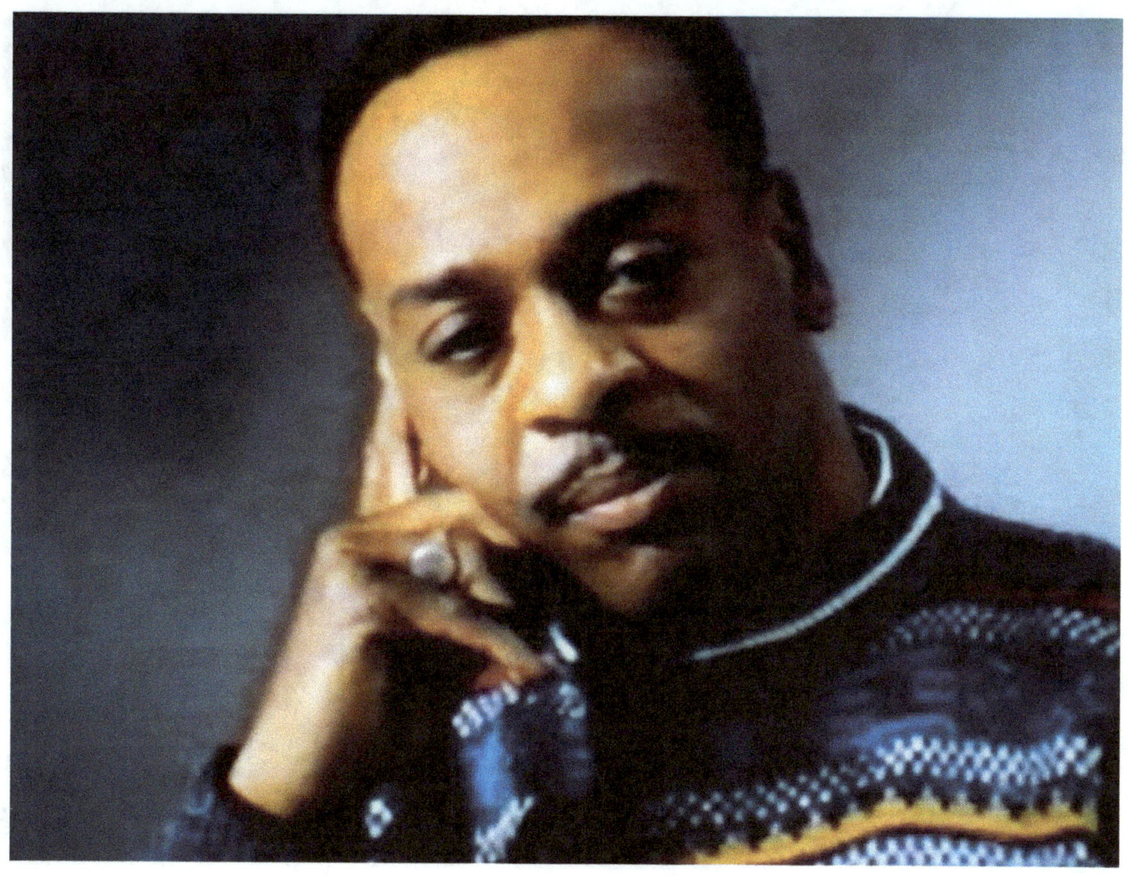

Joseph Plummer as “Dr. Steve Livingston” in “Dual Mania”

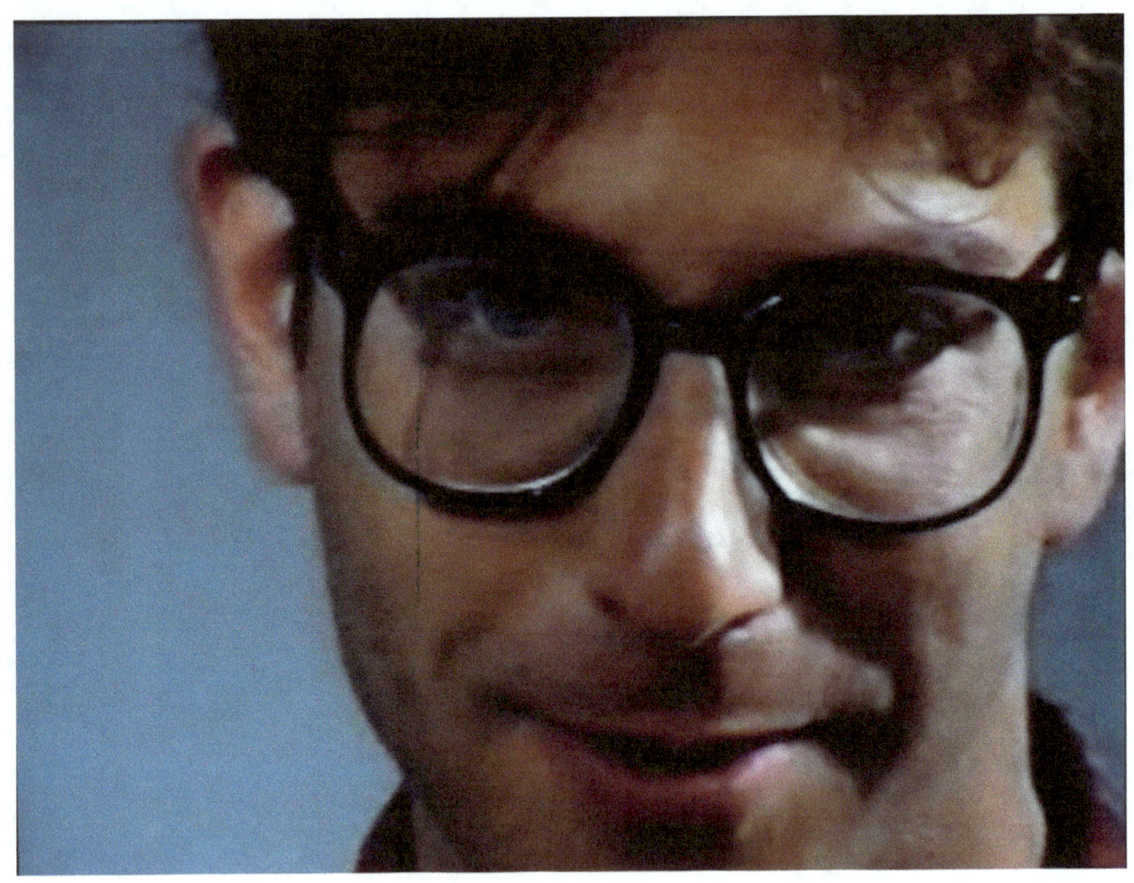

Michael Spitz as “Tommy Valentine” in “Dual Mania”

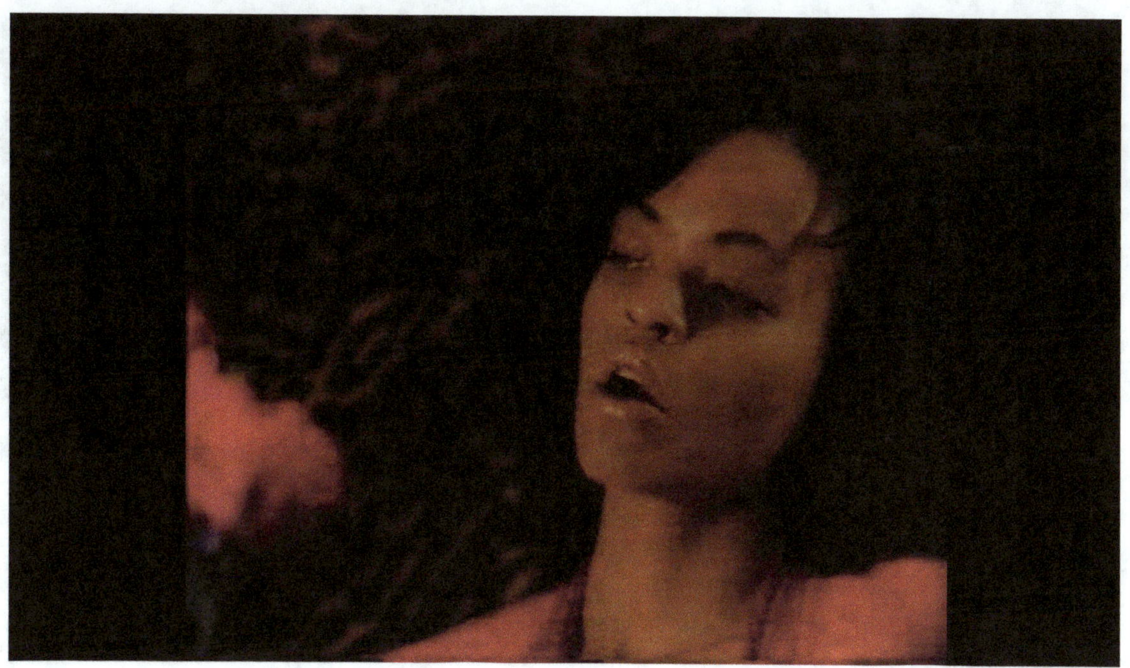

Sherrice Eaglin as “Lydia” in “Dual Mania”

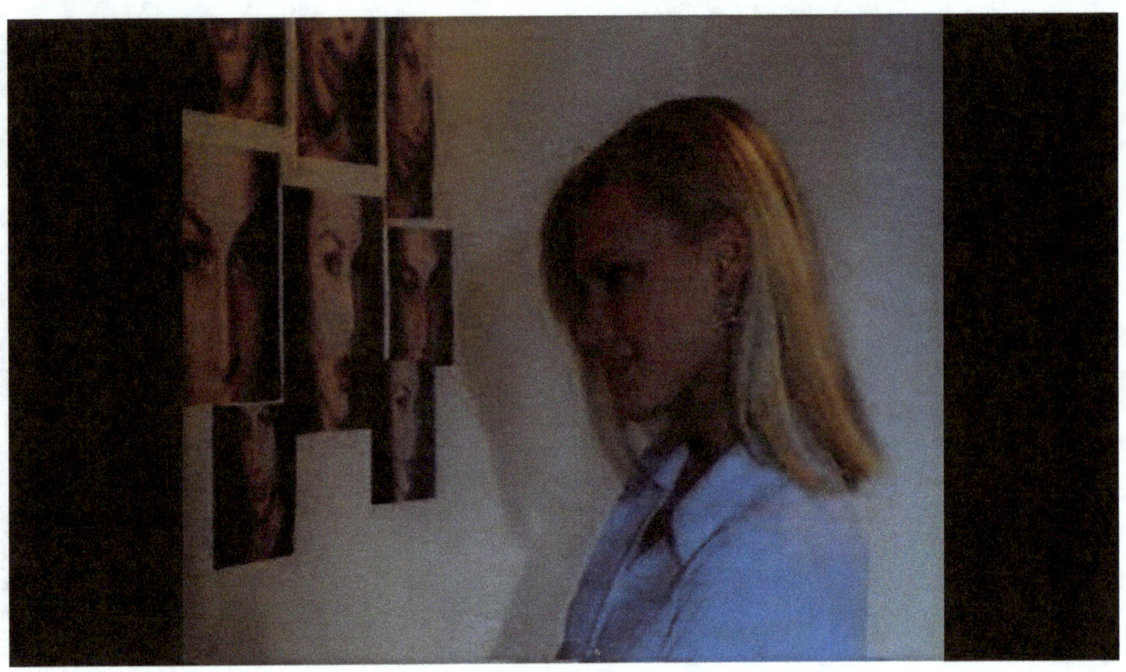

Renee Domenz as "Lucy" in "Dual Mania"

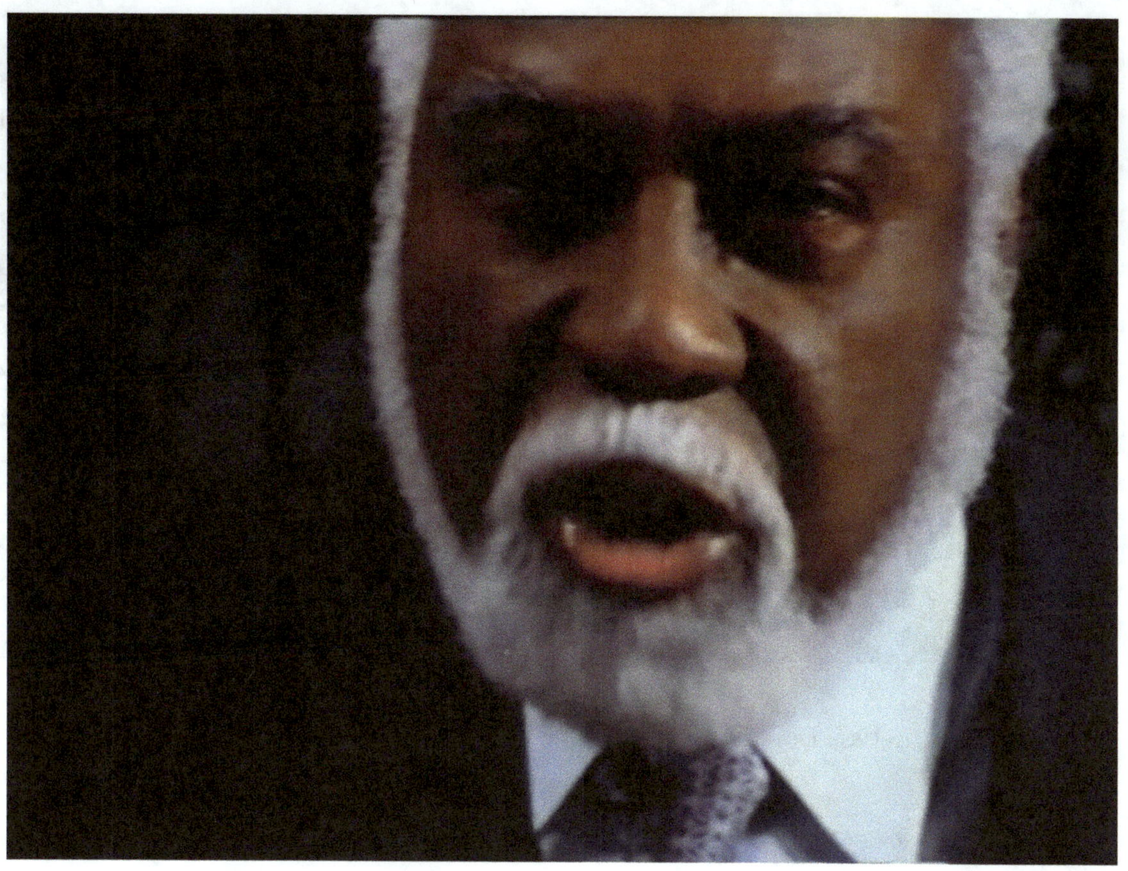

Edgar Douglas as “Dr. Fitzgerald” in “Dual Mania”

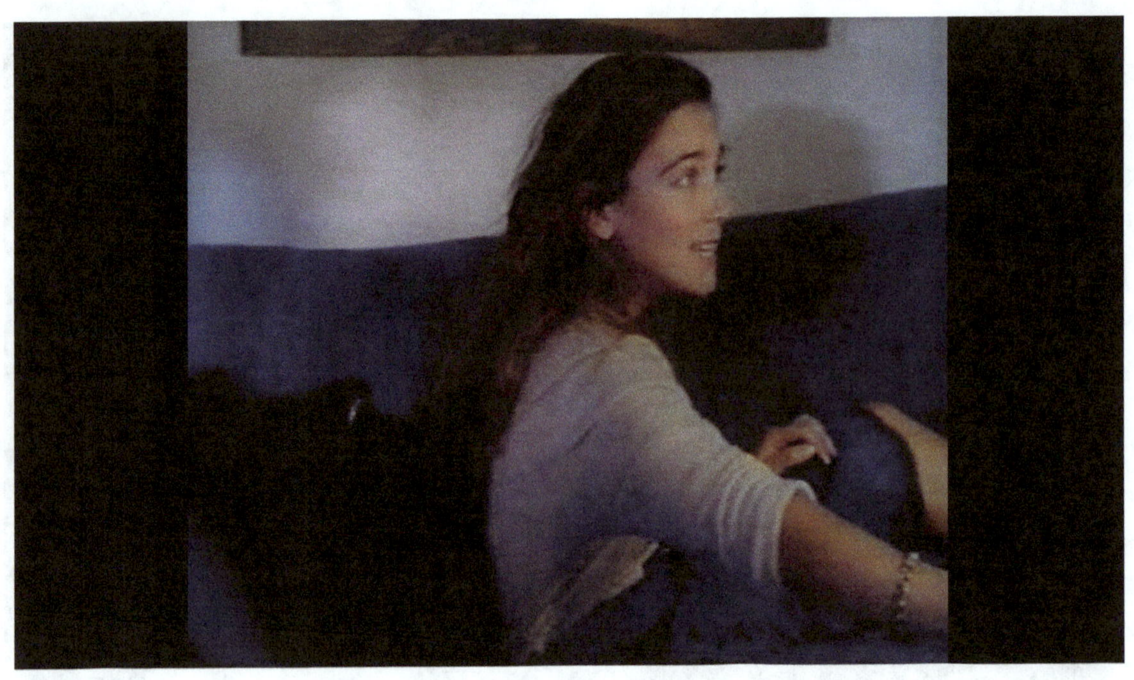

Larissa Borkowski as “Donna Valentine” in “Dual Mania”

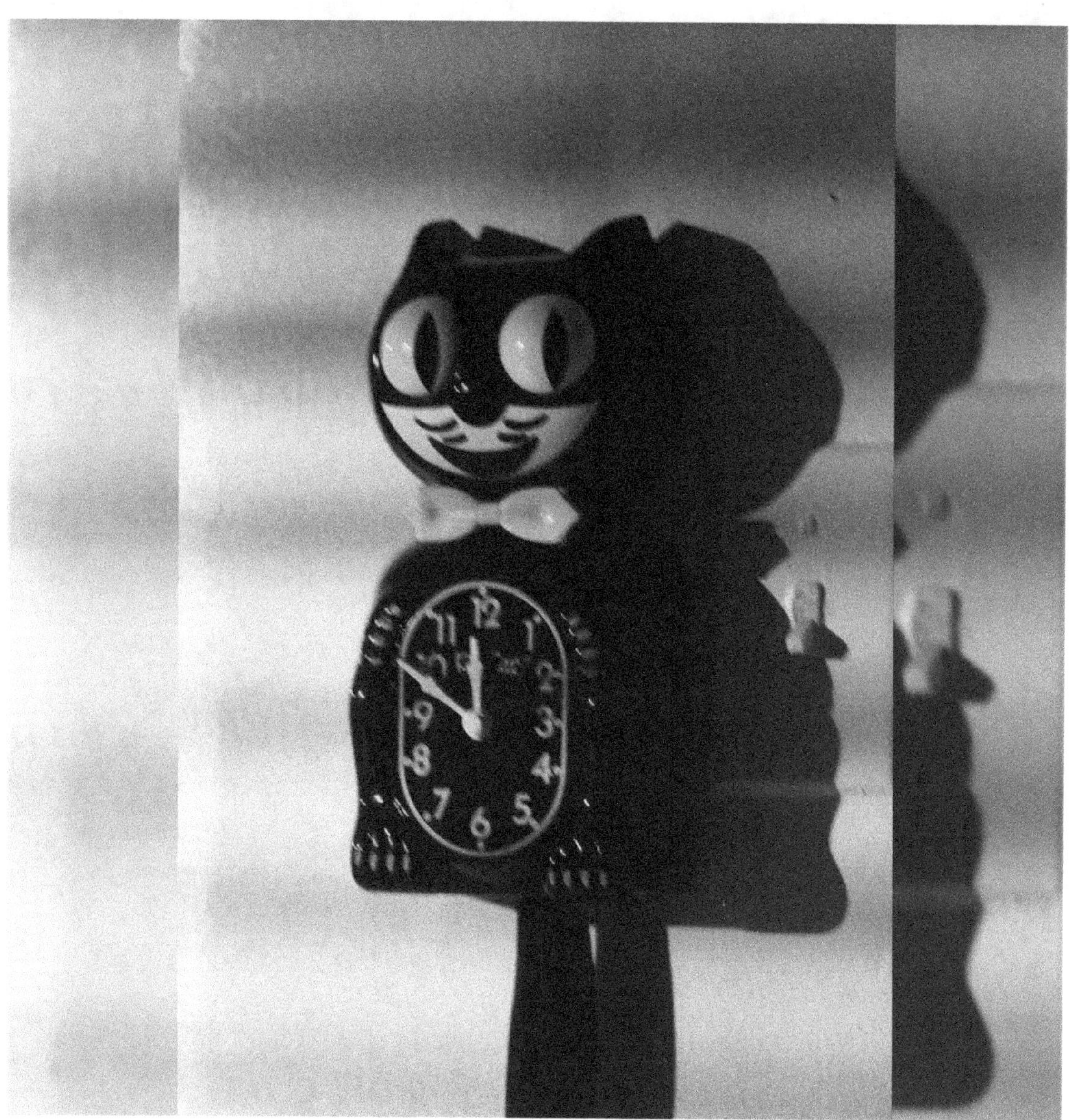

The Famous Kit-Cat Klock in “Dual Mania”

THE AWARDS...

Joseph Strickland,

Dual Mania

&

Cat Ellington

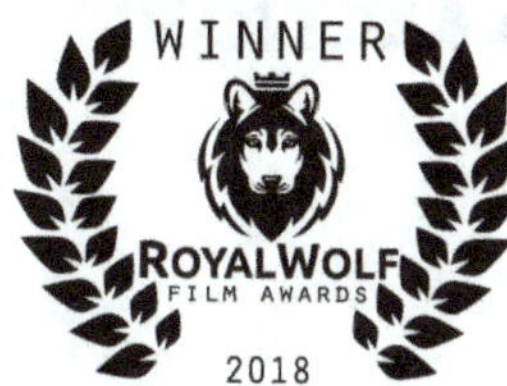

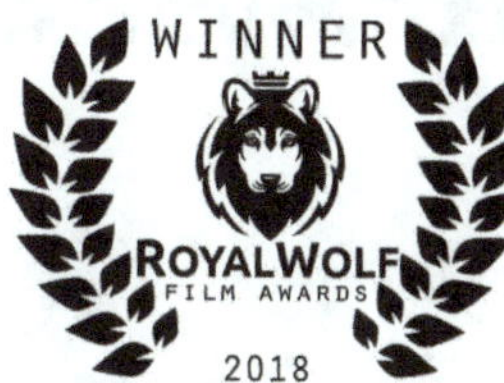

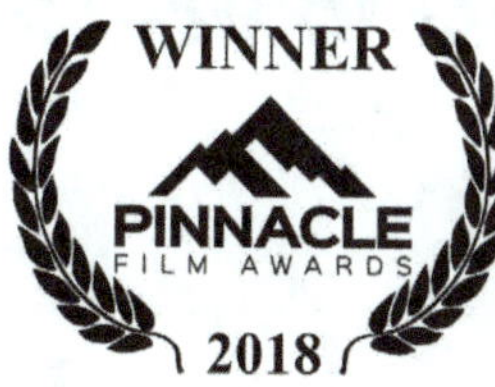

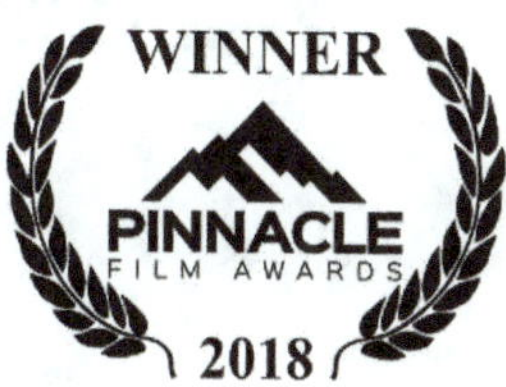

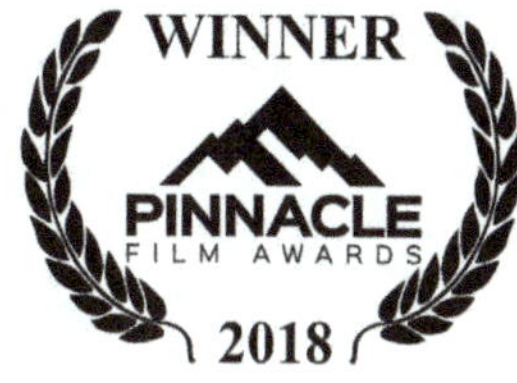

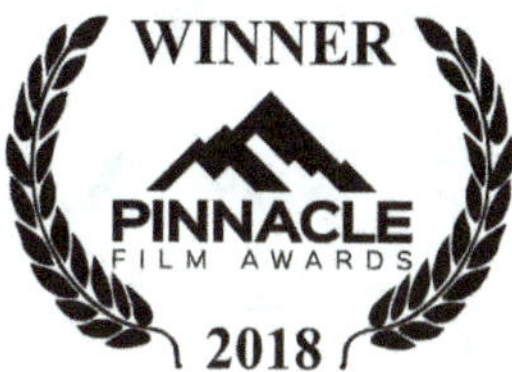

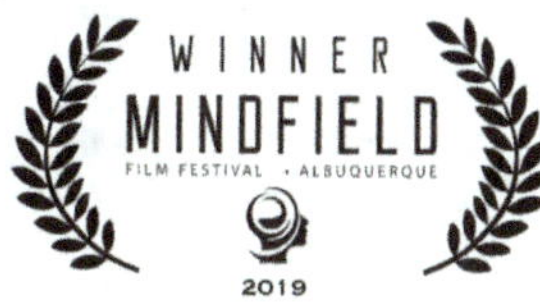

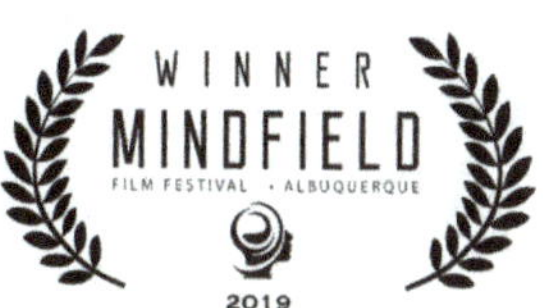

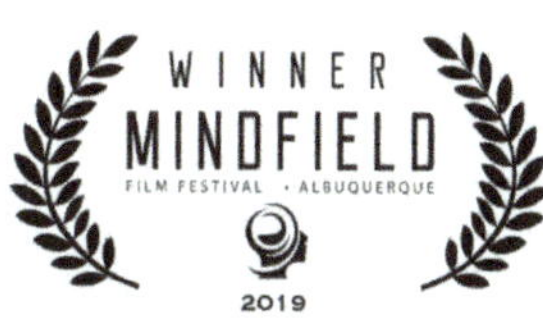

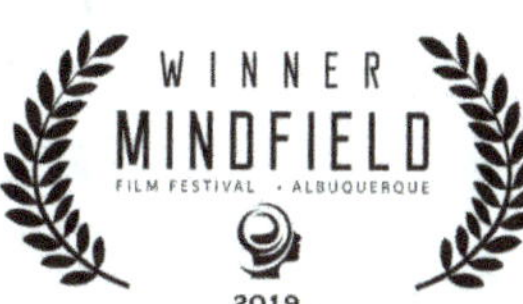

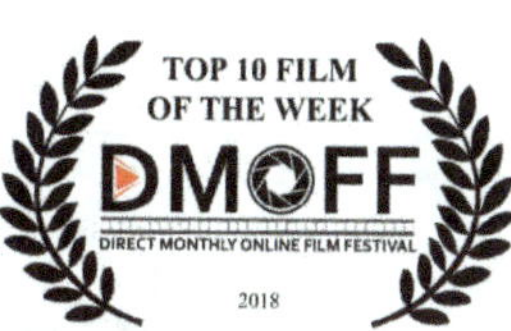

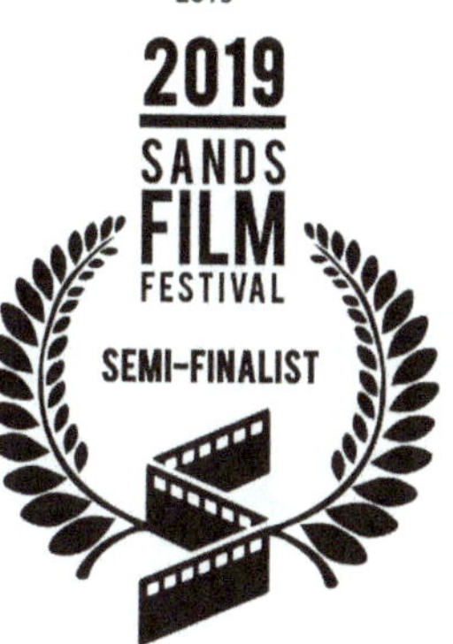

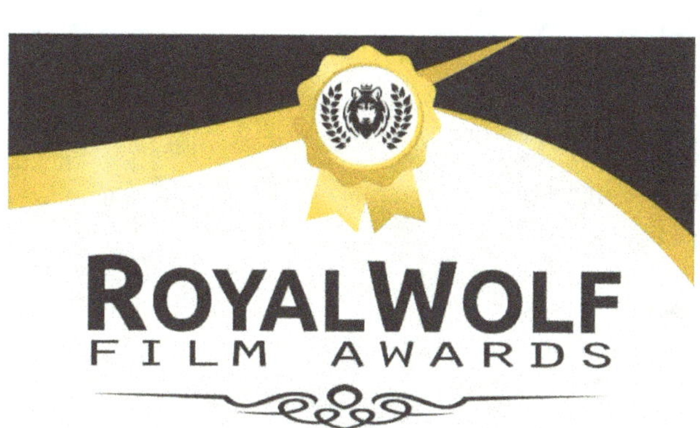

BEST FEATURE FILM - SILVER AWARD
PROUDLY PRESENTED TO

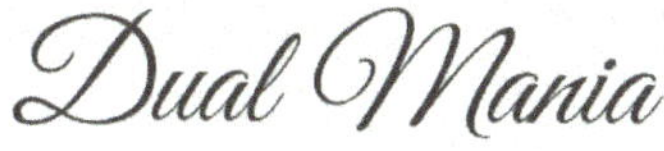

JOSEPH STRICKLAND

IN RECOGNITION OF EXCELLENCE IN FILMMAKING

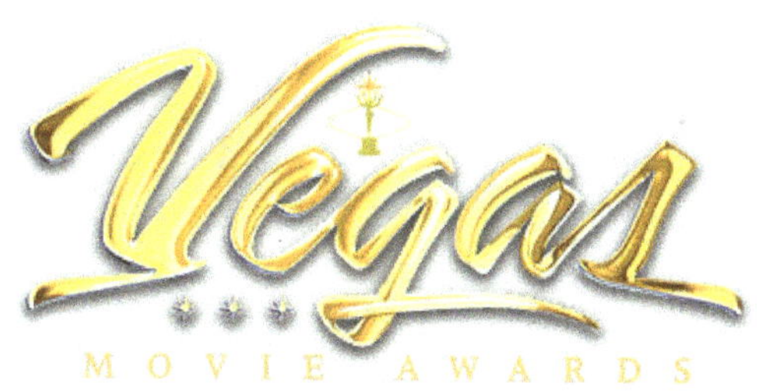

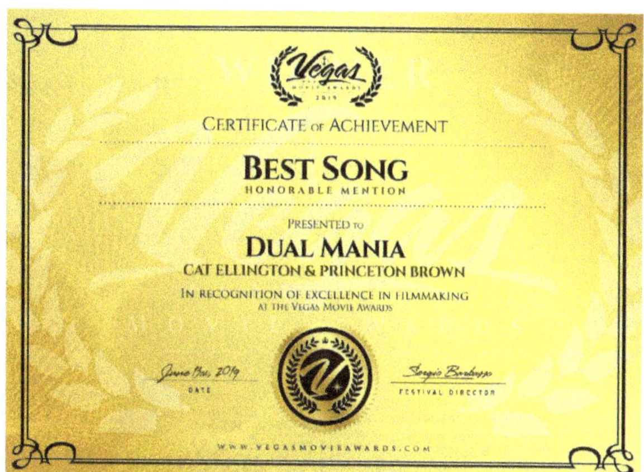

Vegas
MOVIE AWARDS
2019

CERTIFICATE OF ACHIEVEMENT

BEST SONG
HONORABLE MENTION

PRESENTED TO
DUAL MANIA
CAT ELLINGTON & PRINCETON BROWN

IN RECOGNITION OF EXCELLENCE IN FILMMAKING
AT THE VEGAS MOVIE AWARDS

DATE

FESTIVAL DIRECTOR

WWW.VEGASMOVIEAWARDS.COM

The Cat Ellington Sheet Music Collection

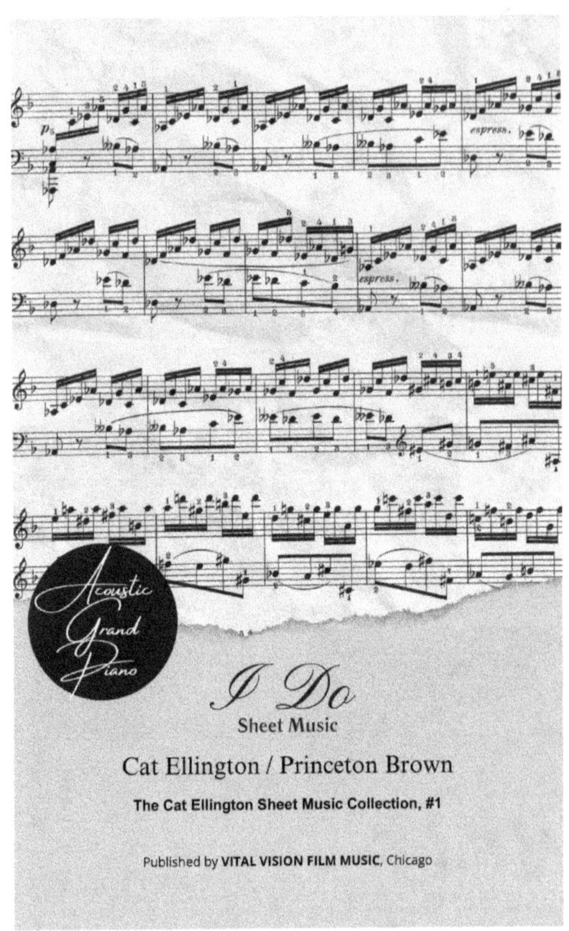

I Do: Sheet Music, Book 1
(Cat Ellington, Princeton Brown)
Publication date: December 3, 2021
Publisher: Vital Vision Film Music

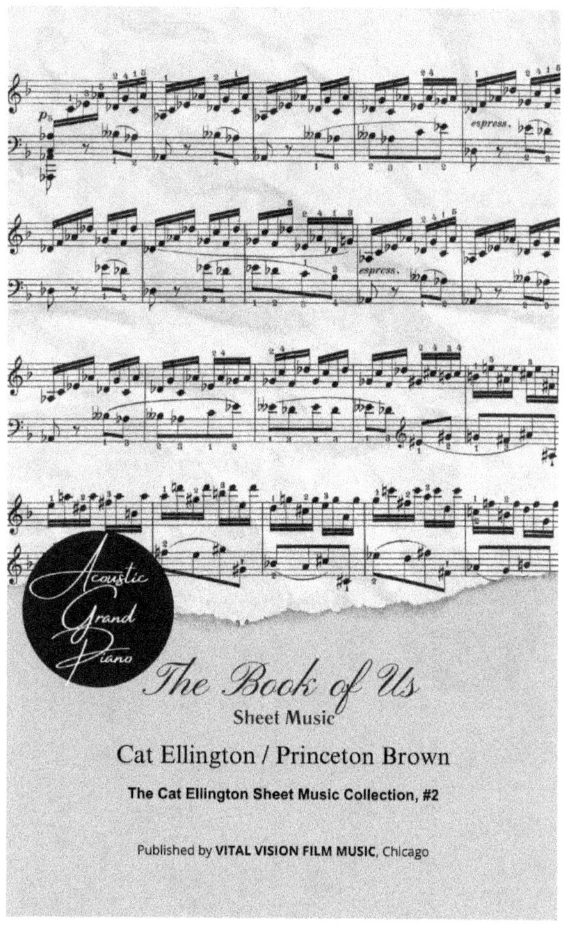

The Book of Us: Sheet Music, Book 2
(Cat Ellington, Princeton Brown)
Publication date: December 3, 2021
Publisher: Vital Vision Film Music

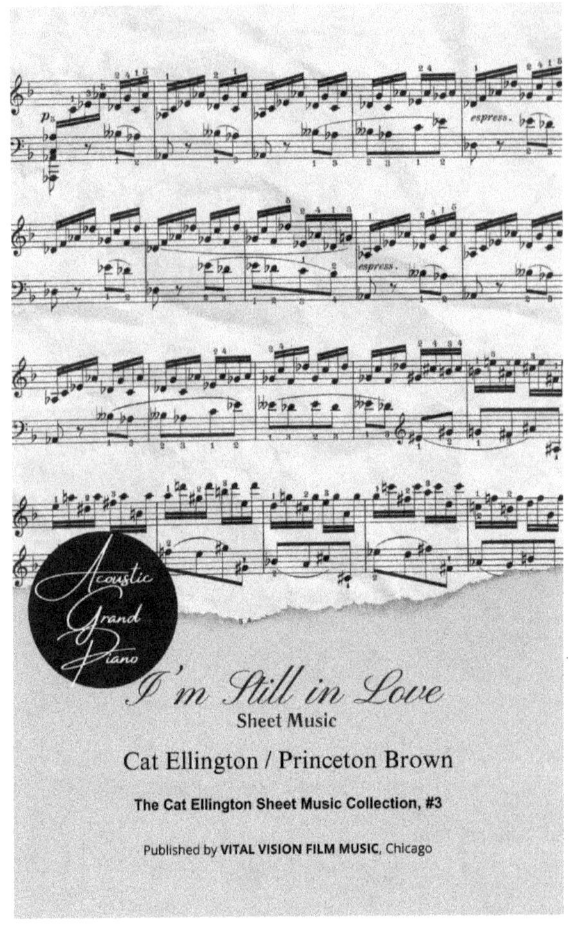

I'm Still in Love: Sheet Music, Book 3
(Cat Ellington, Princeton Brown)
Publication date: December 3, 2021
Publisher: Vital Vision Film Music

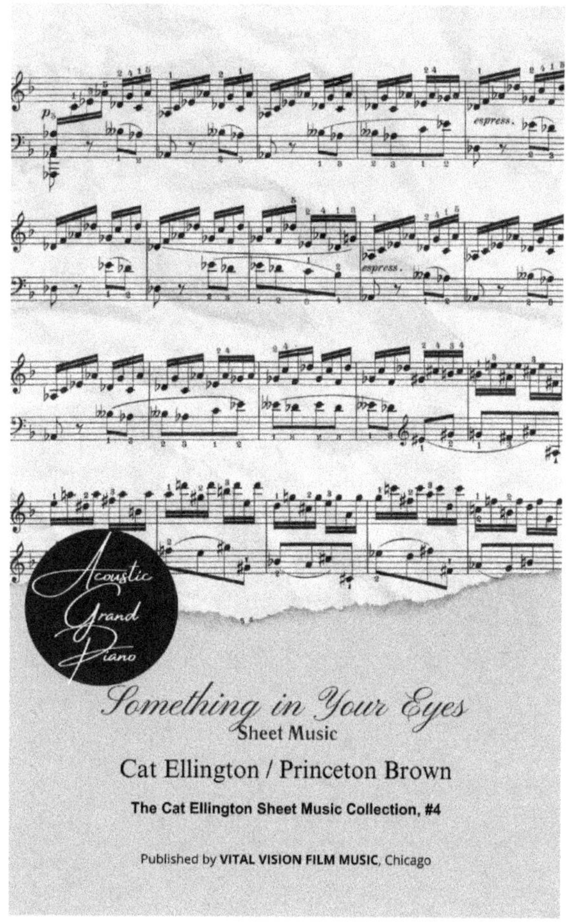

Something in Your Eyes: Sheet Music, Book 4
(Cat Ellington, Princeton Brown)
Publication date: December 3, 2021
Publisher: Vital Vision Film Music

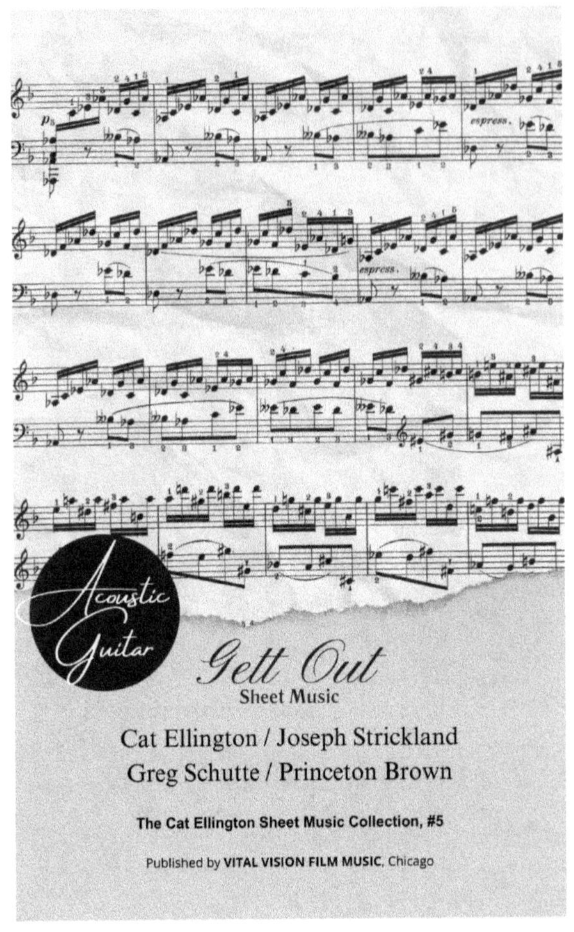

Gett Out: Sheet Music, Book 5
(Cat Ellington, Joseph Strickland, Greg Schutte, Princeton Brown)
Publication date: December 3, 2021
Publisher: Vital Vision Film Music

About the Authors

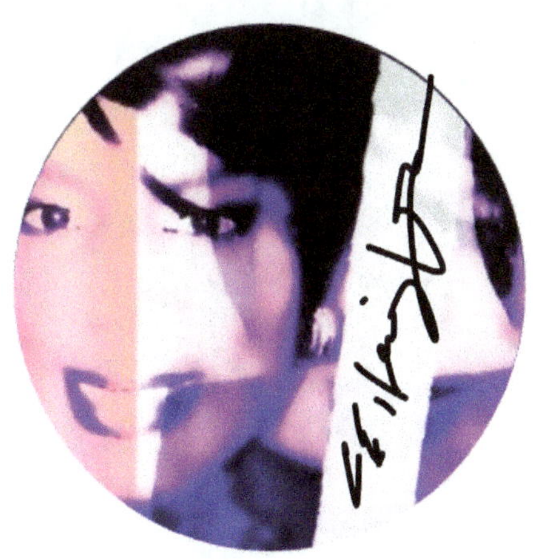

Cat Ellington is an American songwriter, casting director, poet, author, and entrepreneur from Chicago, IL. She is best known for her creative contributions to the diverse industries and fields of music, movies, art, and literature.

Cat Ellington's professional credits list a collection of nonfiction books, including the Reviews by Cat Ellington series, The Making of Dual Mania, More Imaginative Than Ordinary Speech, Memoirs in Gogyohka, and You Can Quote Me On That. In film and music, Ellington's credentials include her work on the psychological thriller, "Dual Mania," and its soundtrack--on which she wrote five original songs: "The Book of Us," "I'm Still in Love," "Something in Your Eyes," "Gett Out," and "I Do."

Outside of her professional element, the award-winning creative enjoys reading, listening to music, cooking, collecting vintage and modern charm bracelets, watching movies and classic TV shows, sailing, jet-skiing, playing tennis, and eating frozen yogurt -- lots of it.

Cat Ellington on Amazon: Books, Biography, Blog, Audiobooks, Kindle

Cat Ellington at the Award-Winning Boutique Domain

Cat Ellington at the Review Period with Cat Ellington

Cat Ellington at IMDb

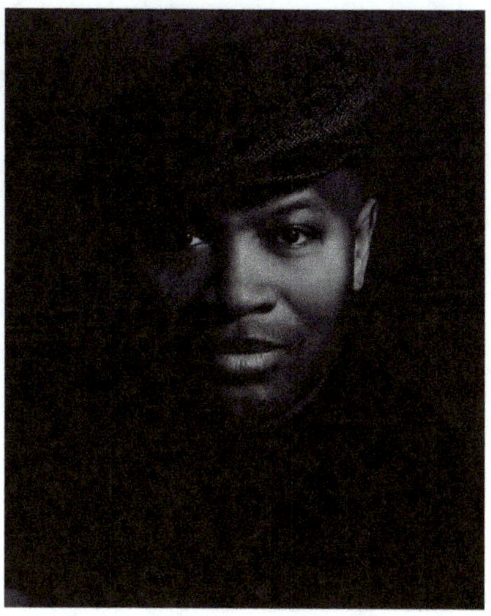

Joseph Strickland is an American film director, screenwriter, producer, and author from Chicago, IL. A former film festival judge for the 32nd Chicago International Film Festival and the 14th Annual Chicago International Children's Film Festival, Strickland also served as Chair of the Features Jury on the adult jury panel for the 15th Annual Chicago International Children's Film Festival.

The Making of Dual Mania: Filmmaking Chicago Style is the author's first collaborative work of nonfiction, co-authored with fellow writer and theater critic B.J. Patterson, and author Cat Ellington, to whom Strickland is married. The fiery narrative was inspired by Strickland's directorial debut *Dual Mania*, a psychological thriller dealing with the dual persona a young possesses and attempts to conceal throughout his ongoing sessions with his therapist.

Outside of his creative work, Strickland enjoys watching Turner Classic Movies (TCM), reading, oil painting, visiting art museums, and watching the Chicago Bears.

Joseph Strickland on Amazon: Books, Biography, Blog, Kindle

Joseph Strickland at The Film Emporium

Joseph Strickland at Goodreads

Joseph Strickland at IMDb

Joseph Strickland at Open Library

About the Producers

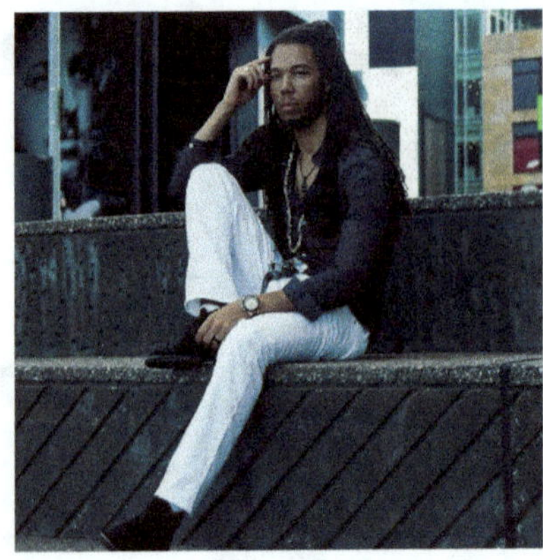

Of Jamaican descent, ***Princeton Brown*** is an LA-based music producer, mixing & mastering engineer, singer-songwriter, and entrepreneur who has his own Princeton Brown Mastering company. His father is a DJ in Jamaica, and his mother is a classical pianist. The co-composer and co-producer of *Instrumentals: Music from the Motion Picture Dual Mania*, Princeton Brown is a native of Minneapolis, Minnesota.

Princeton Brown Mastering

Princeton Brown at IMDb

Princeton Brown on SoundCloud

Princeton Brown on Spotify

Princeton Brown on Apple Music

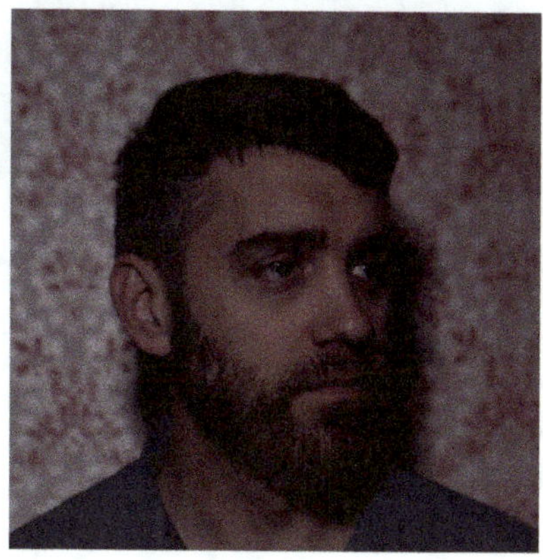

Greg Schutte is an American composer, producer, and performer based out of Minneapolis, MN. Raised on Rock n Roll, Jazz and later steeped in Americana, Soul, Funk, and World Beat, Greg's music is an honest amalgam of his experience and creativity within all of these genres.

Greg Schutte Music

Greg Schutte at IMDb

Greg Schutte on SoundCloud

Greg Schutte on Spotify

Greg Schutte on Apple Music

www.ingramcontent.com/pod-product-compliance
Lightning Source LLC
LaVergne TN
LVHW080248110826
845148LV00023BA/872

* 9 7 9 8 2 1 8 3 6 8 1 2 8 *